Time Flies Whether You're Having Fun . . . Or Not

Times Flies Whether You're Having Fun ... Or Not

MORE STORIES FILLED WITH HUMOR, SPIRIT, AND HOPE
INSPIRATION AND ENTERTAINING

Bob Cushman

Dedication

I would like to dedicate this book to the billions of people on this planet who neither bought nor read It's So Simple . . . It Just Ain't Easy. *You, more than any others, inspired me to write another book. I reasoned if I only sold six hundred of the first book, there must still be a bestseller inside me.*
This could be it!
Or not!

Pre-press work done by:
North Star Press of St. Cloud, Inc.
PO Box 451
St. Cloud, MN 56302

Printed in the United States of America by:
Versa Press, Inc.
East Peoria IL, 61611

Cover design: Bob Cushman

ISBN: 0-9704964-0-0

"We are, in fact, on a journey and have much to learn. From our friends and, even more so, from those not so friendly, we are destined to learn what our souls yearn for. The journey is the process of enlightenment for which we have all gathered. From one another we are receiving that which we are ready to learn. All of us students, Each of us a teacher."
—*The Promise of a New Day*
Karen Casey and Martha Vanceburg

Introduction

I have long been fascinated by stories. Stories of all kinds. It doesn't matter whether they come in the form of a movie, a book, a mother telling a bedtime story to her child, or an old man telling anyone who will listen what it was like in the old days. Stories are the fabric of our lives.

Stories tell us more about the human condition than all the books written about psychology, sociology, theology, anthropology, or any other "ology." When I taught a class on behavioral science, I relied much more on artists, novelists, songwriters, painters, movie-makers, and dramatists (story-tellers all) than I did on theorists to help students understand human behavior. Storytellers outdo the scientists and philosophers in describing the nitty-gritty of what really happens in the world. Stories are not about theory, evidence, and conjecture. Stories are about people, about people's lives, about what people really do.

Before the printing press, storytelling was how learning was passed from generation to generation. Native Americans and other aboriginal cultures continue that tradition even today. Each person is a storyteller. Every person's life is a story. Each person learns from other people's stories. Each

1

person is both student and teacher. And the stories shape our lives.

Consider this story a friend told me one day while we were having coffee: When he was a young boy, Don Anderson sold the Sunday paper on the street corners of Aitkin, Minnesota. Another boy did the same, and they were expected to work different corners. There was, however, one prime corner in this small town, and both boys, being both competitive and ambitious, laid claim to it. Every Sabbath day, the same squabble took place as each boy tried to work the corner alone. Cuss words and name-calling filled the Aitkin air as each cried, "This is my corner."

That, of course, was followed by, "No, it's not. It's mine." Things usually escalated to pushing and shoving, and occasional fisticuffs.

One morning, a stranger happened upon the two boys engaged in their usual Sunday ritual and asked what it was all about. After hearing out each boy, the man simply asked, "Why don't you both work this corner and divvy up the profits?"

The two quickly agreed, and, "This," Don told me, "is how I formed the first of my many business partnerships."

And what is the moral of that story? Where's the significance? Ah, that's the true beauty of stories. I don't know those answers any more than you do. Draw your own conclusions. We could discuss our respective views and quite possibly even agree. But whether we did or not it wouldn't matter. Every person hears the story from a personal perspective, and the conclusions we reach will be formed from our own frame of reference.

I know that the story was very important to Don. This was the beginning of a pattern that was to continue throughout his successful business career. Don's first partner, if he remembers at all, would tell the story quite differently and probably attach to it an entirely different meaning. The stranger is apt to have no memory of the day and most certainly would have no idea how great an impact he had on Don. And I wrote the story a little differently from how Don told it, adding in my own perspective.

Our stories are told from our individual perspectives and reflect the uniqueness of who we are. Each event becomes a mixture of fact and fiction filtered through other experiences of our lives. Facts are seldom of prime importance. What I believe to be important is each nugget of truth gleaned by both the teller and the listener.

When you hear or read someone's stories, you are being invited to have a front row seat at a piece of the drama that has been another's life. You are invited now to take a comfortable seat and pass the time with some of my stories. Time will pass quickly, because time does indeed fly— whether you're having fun or not.

"My health is good,
it's my age that's bad."
—Roy Acuff

"Toto, I don't think
we're in Kansas anymore."
—from *The Wizard of Oz*

Chapter One

A funny thing happened to me on my way to my first book signing for *It's So Simple . . . It Just Ain't Easy*. As a long-time resident of Paynesville, it made sense to have a book signing at a local store. The newest building on the main street, Corner Floral, was an absolutely perfect spot. You couldn't find a more idyllic setting—spacious and filled with the most wonderful sights, sounds, and smells. The store owners, Bob and Sue Brauchler, were more than happy to share their shop with me.

December 16, a Friday, was the date chosen. Everyone had hustled to get the book to the printers in time for an early December release. Books make good Christmas presents. And I love nearly everything about Christmas. I like the snow. I like the crisp, clean air. I like the tinsel and glitter, the colors and bright lights. The songs are so hopeful, joyous, and nostalgic. The Christmas story is a personal favorite. I like the Grinch, elves, Santa Claus, and sleigh bells. The floral shop was alive with a stunning array of flowers and gifts that celebrate all aspects of the season. It was perfect. The book was scheduled for release December 10, plenty of time to get books to the store.

4

I knew Christmas. I knew mid-December was a great time for a book signing. I knew the floral shop was the right place. What I didn't know was the printing business. Boy, did I not know the printing business! Oh, I know a lot more now, but . . . what I least understood about the printing game was a printer's concept of time. When a printing company says it will have a book off the press and ready for delivery on December 10, they don't really mean December 10 at all; what they mean is, with luck, the book will be ready sometime this millennium.

Having spent my career working in schools that are run strictly by clocks, bells, and calendars, I was silly enough to think that December 10 meant . . . oh, I don't know . . . maybe . . . uh . . . well, December 10, I guess. It seemed like such a logical assumption at the time. So much so, in fact, that it had even seemed reasonable to schedule the signing for the sixteenth. Nearly a week's grace seemed generous.

On Monday, the fifth, Mary and I drove to St. Cloud to check with my editors (mentors and friends, too), Corinne and Rita Dwyer. They informed us the book wouldn't be coming off the press until the twelfth. Okay. Don't panic. That still leaves a four-day cushion. On the ninth day, they further informed me that special arrangments were being made, and the book was scheduled to be delivered to their St. Cloud office at 1:00 P.M. on Friday the sixteenth.

Now our leeway is down from six days to five hours. We can deal with that. No problem yet. Nothing to worry about. There's still a comfortable grace period. St. Cloud is only a half-hour drive. So I will pick up a couple boxes of books at one o'clock on Friday afternoon and have them at the floral shop in plenty of time to set up and be ready for the signing at six. A phone call Wednesday told me the books left the printers in Illinois on time and would be in Minneapolis Thursday night.

Now we are in business.

I slept late on Thursday. I lingered over breakfast and lounged around the house for a couple hours reading the paper, doing the daily crossword and a few other life-ofleisure activites that had become my routine since I'd quit at school. Morning had become "me time." Household chores and writing could wait for afternoon. Mornings were mine. That particular morning included a little meditation and reverie. About 11:30 A.M., I started thinking about the many things I needed to do to get ready for my big day on Friday. That's when it hit me.

It felt like someone with heavy work boots kicked me in the chest—a heavy, dull thud right in the breast bone. I began to sweat and my left arm felt numb. I knew what was happening, but denial is such an old friend he jumped in immediately. "NO! You are not having a heart attack. You can't have a heart attack. Not now. Not with the book signing tomorrow night." I took two aspirin and sat down to rest. The pain subsided rather quickly. "See," denial assured me, "just a little anxiety attack."

I drove to the grocery store to get the Christmas napkins and paper cups we needed for Friday's festivites. When I returned home, I was gasping for breath. I put the stuff on the counter and sat down on the couch to rest. In a few minutes, BAM! It hit me again. This jolt was a little less intense. A bit more scattered. Along with my chest pain, my neck and shoulders ached. My head hurt. Again, the numbness in my arm. Again, the denial. "You're probably catching a cold. Or getting a touch of the flu. That's it! You're getting the flu." More aspirin. I rested. The pain eased. So I put on my jacket and drove to a local restaurant to get the Christmas cookies we had ordered for Friday. I had to get everything and make sure it was all in place. After all, my book was due tomorrow. A truckload of them was somewhere between Illinois and Minneapolis at this very time. I was really tired by the time I got the cookies into the house. *Really* tired. I sat again. I was soaked in sweat. The third jolt hit me. Hard. Denial is one thing. Utter stupidity is something else. I drove myself to the local hospital. It was 2:00 P.M.

Now it was time to panic.

"I am here to live out loud."
Emile Zola

"You can either keep pedaling,
get off the bike, or fall over."
Really Important Stuff My
Kids Have Taught Me
Cynthia Copeland Lewis

Chapter Two

The nurses in the emergency room were wonderful. The doctors were great. I got terrific care. The diagnosis was, as expected, a heart attack. On Friday, I was transferred to the St. Cloud Hospital where the coronary care staff took over. They decided angioplasty was the way to go, put the balloon in, and sent me back to recovery. I don't want to dwell on the treatment. I was sleeping most of the time, and I don't understand any of it anyway. What they can and do accomplish in modern medicine blows me away. I marvel at the skill and dedication of those folks who choose medicine. Suffice it to say that everyone did their job superbly. I couldn't have had better care, and I am extremely grateful to them for knowing their stuff. Once again, I owe my life to the medical staffs in both Paynesville and St. Cloud. Thank you, one and all.

I want to tell of some other things I believe were important to my recovery. First of all, I quit smoking. Shortly after the doctor walked into the emergency room that Thursday, he asked if I was a smoker. I told him I had been. "How long has it been," he asked, "since you've had a cigarette?"

"About three hours," I told him.

Not original, but true. Actually, I stole the line from my brother.

My history with nicotine is classic. It reveals how incredibly stupid I can be. Everything I understand about addiction I can find in my own love affair with tobacco. I'll tell that story later. As of this writing, let the record show I haven't had a cigarette for nearly six years. I am as proud of that as I am ashamed of the forty-five years I smoked. I am convinced that my not smoking has as much to do with my current health as anything.

The other healthy life-style choice I've made is to exercise on a regular basis. I am currently trying to get thirty minutes on the treadmill each day. I bought a bicycle and ride that during nice weather, and I use the stationary bike when it is not so nice. And I am trying to eat a healthier diet, but I have more trouble sticking to that than I do the exercise regimen.

I have long been a believer that healing is as much a spiritual process as it is a physical one. Following my colon cancer surgery in 1983, I didn't really start to heal until my daughter, Jodi, came to visit me. I had been scheduled to go home a week after the second operation. The doctors had done all that they could, and it was matter of waiting for my organs to start functioning properly. Over two weeks went by and we were still waiting. Each day Dr. Tims would listen to my stomach, shake his head and tell me he couldn't understand why he wasn't hearing any bowel sounds.

I had told my kids to wait until I was out of the hospital to come and visit. I had figured we would have more time together after I got home than we would while I was cooped up in a hospital room. Logical thinking. I'm usually too damn logical. Mary realized this to be a big mistake and secretly arranged for Jodi to fly home and surprise me. On a Sunday evening, Jodi popped into my hospital room, and I have never been happier to see anyone. I wept for joy. I laughed harder than I had for weeks. Hearty laughter and tears come from the same pool deep inside us—from the very center of our being—and are the deepest feelings we share. Sharing those depths is, indeed, a spiritual experience. And that's the gift Jodi gave me that Sunday.

On Monday the doctor heard bowel sounds, and I was home that Friday. No one will ever convince me that Jodi's visit wasn't what I most needed to start the healing process. There had been, to be sure, the combined skills of the surgeons, the wonderfully caring nurses, and all the other staff people at the hospital. There had been an outpouring of love and concern from scores of people—family, friends, neighbors, and acquaintances—but it wasn't until Jodi showed up, and my spirit began to heal, that I truly started getting better physically.

Similar things happened following the heart attack. My circle of friends was even larger now, and the cards, phone calls, visits, and other expressions of love were huge. The same medical expertise was available. The hospital stay this time was short. My stubbornness and my eagerness to distribute the book had me out before the doctors wanted me to leave. I was up and about anyway and physically doing okay. But I certainly wasn't well. A phone call from Jodi and a letter from my son, Mark, were exactly what I needed.

Jodi's message was brief. "Dad," she said, "you can't die because I want you to help with Megan's graduation party." Megan, our granddaughter was seven at the time. And I will help with that graduation. I knew that before I hung up.

Mark's letter is a tad longer, which is unusual because he normally delivers the cryptic message, and Jodi tends to ramble a bit, like her dad. I asked Mark's permission to print his letter verbatim because it was such a powerful message of spirit and humor that it deserves full attention. Besides I have for years wanted to collaborate with him on a book, and it looks like this is as close as we'll get.

Marks letter:

Dad:

First off I'll get the selfish stuff out of the way.— DAMNIT, DAD!!! You scared the *hell* out of me! What would I do without you in my life? You can't go around frightening those of us who love you like this. It's Christmas for God's sake.

Okay, Now I feel better. Let's work on you. Listen to the doctors. They have experience in these matters and tools to help you. Get better. I pray that you do.

You've been very good at giving advice. Now I'd like you to take some. You know—whether you believe it or not—that by being born a human you have earned the right to experience unreasonable happiness. You especially, the man who has brought happiness and peace to so many.

Do you experience those things? Because the source of these feelings is such a great healer if you allow it to be. The spirit can off almost anything, but it doesn't like being ignored. The soul will speak, but when the mind is plugging its ears, stomping its feet and chanting,

"NA-NA, NA-NA, NA-NA. I CAN'T HEAR YOU. LA, LA-LA. LA, LA-LA. HMM. HMM. HMM."

The soul might just let you know in some other way. Maybe it's a sign from the universal mind that it's the dawn of the anniversary of one of the greatest healers and teachers (Hmm. Do those occupations sound familiar?) You should be listening more to your higher self and work toward achieving "BOBNESS." Be selfish for a while. Do what you love and don't worry about what you're supposed to do. Be Bob. Feel Bob's pain and let it go. Visualize Bobness in its purest light. Live . . . Love . . . Laugh. That's all there is to do. Your higher self (along with the doctors) can put Humpty back together again.

Be Bob. Don't just do Bob . . . *Be* Bob. Live Bob to the fullest. I know I can't make everything better for you, (I lost my job as a band-aid) but the human, the great Spirit. (Apologies to Robert Heinlein for paraphrased plagiarism.) The two are one and, with love, are all. (Again apologies, but this time to Alexander Dumas.) I wish for you Godspeed in healing and in health. You are a wonderful human and a great Dad. I believe in you. (Apologies to Tinkerbell.) Do you believe in magic? (Apologies to John Sebastian.) Yes, you do . . . but do you believe you believe in magic? Ah, there's the rub. (Apologies to William Shakespeare—and my massage therapist.) Listen to your doctors—your medicine men— and your friends. Good people do good and mean well. Magician, heal thyself. (Apologies to Socrates or whoever the hell said this.) I love you so much. Get well. Be well. Today is not a good day to die. (Apologies to Little Big Man.) You have good work yet to do. I love you and will be in touch again soon. [Stage direction: Touch your heart.] 'I'll be right there.' (Apologies to *E.T.*)"

How can you not get better with help like that?

Before I leave this thought process, I want to acknowledge another piece of magic that arrived from my friends, Charles and Renee King. They sent me two cards. The first struck me so funny that it had to have triggered some healing endorphins.

> The outside read:
> "You are to friendship what Einstein was to science . . .
> What Michelangelo was to art . . .
> And what Beethoven was to music!"
> And inside:
> "Plus you aren't dead. I love you for that."

To this Charles added:

> "This is quite possibly the tackiest card I've sent anybody—which tells me something about the boundaries of our friendship! I cleared the card section laughing over this one. . . . Hope it brings the same kind of laughter to you."

It did, Charles. And it helped so much to laugh during those days. I am so very grateful to all my friends and family for helping me through. We shared many laughs and much joy.

The Kings' second card was very touching. It pictured an eagle and had this verse:

11

"May the Great Spirit grant you the strength of eagle's wings,
The faith and courage to fly to new heights,
And the wisdom to rely on His spirit to carry you there."

And they called it a "You Are Already Well" card and reminded me that I have always had the qualities of strength, faith, courage, and wisdom.

My recovery—from cancer, the heart attack, and every other pitfall I've had—is about all these things. I am so very thankful for all the professional people without whose skill, knowledge, and expertise I couldn't have made it. But I am equally in debt to the friends and family members who, throughout my entire sixty-five years, have helped me learn about love and courage and laughter and faith and hope and serenity and all those other things that make up whatever wisdom I have attained

I survived the heart attack, in part, because of what I had learned in surviving the cancer. I outlived the cancer partly because of what I learned toughing out the divorce. What I had learned in my dysfunctional family helped me endure the divorce. And so on and so on.

"Don't confuse the
specter of your origin
with your present worth"
Splinter in a *Teenage
Mutant Ninja Turtle* movie

Chapter Three

I am a survivor. I like, since I use the skills and scars received in the heat of battle, to refer to myself as a wounded healer. And I like to identify with the trees known as fire-origin-species. Several years ago in the Paynesville High School teacher's lounge, a biology teacher was talking about the different varieties of coniferous trees. He explained to those of us more interested in the previous night's ball scores than anything scientific that when the cones fall off the jack-pine, for example, they are sealed shut so the seeds can't tumble out. These cones just lie on the forest floor for five, ten, twenty, fifty years—until there is a fire. At that time the intense heat melts the seals, and the seeds are released to seek fertile soil in which to grow. Fascinating. How things happen in the natural world is a constant source of amazement to me. These trees, which require a fire to find renewed life, are called fire-origin species.

What a great name! So descriptive. And appropriate: fire-origin species. A tree that finds rebirth, growth, and strength in a tragedy. And what a wonderful name for all of us who have been burned by life and discover personal growth in that experience. Survivors of our own personal holocausts. What a fabulous concept! Probably applies to all of us, huh? Our pain can be the key to our healing. Wait a minute. Disclaimer needed. We have all been burned by life at some time or another, but some choose to remain victims. The name doesn't fit for those who choose to cling to their resentments and remain victims because, for them, there is then no new origin—no re-beginning—that rises like the Phoenix from the ashes.

But if the seed has found fertile ground, and you have found new life and new dreams, then you belong in this distinguished group—fire-origin-species.

Congratulations. My hat is doffed to you. Stand tall. Be proud. The seed has become you, and you now have the responsibility to determine its (your) fate. Nurture the seed. Water, as needed, with your tears. Allow it to grow at its own pace. Take special care with your seed-self. It needs the strength and care of others along the way. It may even need a little fertilizer on occasion.

You are the gardener and the plant.

As I wrote this short chapter I couldn't help but think of the song, "Seeds," that Kathy Matea recorded on her CD, *Lonesome Standard Time*. It was written by Pat Alger and Ralph Murphy. The lyric reminds us we're all just seeds.

> "Sometimes I stop on my way home
>   And watch the children play
>   And I wonder if they wonder
>   What they'll be someday.
>   Some will dream a big dream
>   And make it all come true
>   While others go on dreaming
>   Of things they'll never do.
> (Chorus)
> We're all just seeds in God's hands
>   We start the same
>   But where we land
>   Is sometimes fertile soil
>   And sometimes sand.
>   We're all just seeds
>   In God's hands.

14

I saw a friend the other day
    I hardly recognized.
    He'd done a lot of living
    Since I'd last looked in his eyes.
    He told his tale of how he'd failed
    The lessons he'd been taught
    But he offered no excuses
    And he left me with this thought . . .
(Chorus)
And as I'm standing
    At a Crossroads once again
    I'm reminded we're all the same when we begin
    And in the end . . .
(Chorus)

May your seed-self grow tall like the jack pine, ever reaching for the sun.

And may you, as Karen Kaiser-Clark taught me, "grow deep, not just tall."

Chapter Four

When I was in the early stages of learning about the operating rules and roles in a shame-based or dysfunctional family system, I mapped out my own family to test the theories. It was a perfect match. The roles are fuzzier for me now, but they seemed quite clear to me at that time. My own role seemed to be the hero, but it is a role I evolved into.

My older brother, Jack, was the classic scapegoat. Everything that went wrong was, somehow, Jack's fault. It mattered not that most events were far removed from any influence he might have had. He responded in classic scapegoat fashion. He rebelled. Against everyone. He smoked, he drank. He cut school. He got into fights. He developed a reputation as a tough guy. He got thrown in jail a couple times, once for hitting a cop. He did what scapegoats do.

I started out as a mascot. I decided, for whatever reason—or for no reason—that my job was to protect my mom. And I think I performed that task admirably. There are as many styles of mascoting as there are people who assume the role. Some are super-cute. Some have a knack for little screw-ups at just the right moment. Others choose to make people laugh. Many are adept at all of these, and more.

he effort is the same—to

a frail little thing, skinny
ital a half-dozen times with
years of age. People don't
ht when they have a sickly
f age, I had developed asth-
inipulate parents. I got out
promise Dad I'd mow the
I was back in the house
ished my work, I always
recovered enough to go play ball or go swimming. It was
great. Never had to do any chores I didn't like.

My bedroom was next to Mom and Dad's, and, whenever I heard raised voices or harsh words coming from their
bedroom, I would wake up and traipse in announcing
solemnly, "I can't breathe." Mom immediately led me back to
my bed and lay me down. She'd get the Vicks, Mentholatum,
or Ben Gay (we always had every patent medicine in our
medicine cabinet) and begin rubbing my chest and/or back.
She would talk soothingly as she administered the balm,
and I would eventually fall back to sleep.

But never before Dad did.

And that's how I protected my mom. I would somehow
interrupt every argument before it escalated. It worked
beautifully. That is until April 4, 1946. That's the day my little sister, Joy, was born. Suddenly the techniques I had
mastered to get attention didn't work. I'd wheeze around the
house as usual, but Mom was too busy feeding, bathing,
changing, or cuddling the baby. Life became even more con-
fusing for me. All of the skills I had so painstakingly honed
into art forms were being wasted. So I switched gears. I tried
to emulate my brother's scapegoat behaviors. I started
smoking and hanging around with a tougher group. I got in
fights. I started drinking. But I couldn't be bad enough. If I
got kicked out of school, Jack got thrown in jail. He was too
good at being bad. I couldn't compete.

I had to try yet another tack. I began to take some hero-
ic-type risks. I got involved in some school activities. I got on

the school paper and received some positive feedback for the articles I wrote. That seemed pretty neat, so I joined the yearbook staff. This too worked well for me. I was evolving into the family hero without knowing it. I went to college. I was the first person in the family to do that. I took a high profile job as a radio announcer at a local station. Now, by God, when people in Minot heard the name Cushman, they are likely to think of my accomplishments rather than my dad's drinking or my brother's escapades.

I had become a full-fledged family hero.

"Life is amazing, isn't it? One minor
character takes some action and the
whole world turns upside down."
Van Johnson's character
in the Woody Allen movie,
Purple Rose of Cairo.

Chapter Five

My sister changed everything. Forever. For some reason I
will never fathom, as my sister grew, my dad totally changed,
and the way the family functioned changed with him. Jack
and I each eventually moved away, and that was a factor,
too. Joy's description of growing up is one hundred and
eighty degrees polarized from how either Jack or I describe
our childhood. Our story is totally foreign to her. We might
just as well be telling her some African mythology.

But I want to expand on how Joy changed my life. I was
blind sided by this. While it was happening, I had no idea
how significant she was to be in my life. As usual I chose to
focus on that which made me unhappy. I perceived only how
things effected me. Like most eleven-year olds, I saw only
with my egocentric eyes—not a good way to look when one's
eyes are as non-convergent as mine.

The bigger picture was way beyond me.

In my stream of consciousness, Joy was a big pain in the
butt. A really cute one, but a pest nevertheless. Mom went
back to work when Joy was still a baby, and I got stuck with
the job of baby-sitting. I had to feed her. I had to change her
messy diapers. I had to put her to bed. I had to read to her,

to entertain her. I had to clean up her messes and nurse her when she was sick. I had to, in effect, be both mom and dad to her. They were both working, and Jack was too old for this type of thing.

But so was I. Taking care of a baby is not the way a budding teenager wants to spend his evenings. During school, I was responsible for her from four in the afternoon until her bedtime. On weekends and during summer vacations, my duties were expanded. I took on more responsibility because Mom and Dad both slept late. I became chief cook (Okay. I put cereal in a bowl for breakfast and heated a can of Campbell's soup for lunch. I was eleven. Gimmee a break.), valet, housekeeper, and recreation director. I never would have made it if it hadn't been for our dog, Major.

Major was an eighty-five-pound Springer spaniel. A huge dog and the toughest one in all of northwest Minot. Over the years, I saw him intimidate German shepherds, Alaskan huskies, and every other canine who came around. He also scared the daylights out of mailmen, meter readers, delivery people, and other intruders to 314 Ninth Street. He was a lovable bear of a dog who was fiercely protective of our family, especially Joy. I learned early in the game that Major could be counted on for two things: he would never, ever leave Joy's side when she was outside, and he would keep her out of harm's way. Once those things sunk into my brain, taking care of Joy became considerably less a burden.

When she was outside playing I could forget about her and let Major take over my duties. She was perfectly safe from the neighborhood bullies or any one else who might wish to hurt her. No one messed with Major. If any danger loomed, Major was there. And if I needed Joy home, I simply went to the porch and whistled. Within seconds, Major would pop up from wherever they were, and I'd walk over and bring her home. He was a great baby-sitter, and I was too stupid to realize that what I was doing wasn't really such a good idea. There were, I realized later, dangers Major could not have kept her from. But there was a Higher Power on duty, too, and no harm came to either.

Thus, Major and I raised Joy. And I think we did a pretty good job. She is a wonderful woman and has been one of my dearest friends for the past forty years or so. That, of course, is one of the hidden benefits I wrote of earlier. I know the depth of our friendship was founded in those years I dreaded so much.

And there's more.

When my daughter, Jodi, was born, both her mother and I set sail on uncharted seas. Like all new parents, we bumbled our way through each unexpected event. Kris had a lot of baby-sitting experience, which left her as competent as any new mother. And her mother, who had tons of experience, was only a phone call away. But the surprise in the mix was me. I knew how to change a diaper. I could even bathe a baby. I was pretty good at nurturing, and I spoke baby language. Everything I learned taking care of Joy was still stored in the recesses of my brain and available at my beckoning.

I was a father of the nineties—and it was only 1957. I was able to be with my children as infants and as toddlers, youngsters, and teens. The experiences I had dreaded when I was eleven and twelve became the cornerstone of the relationship I was able to establish with both Jodi and Mark. I was able to build upon, with my own kids, what I had learned with my baby sister. I look back upon what I had loathed so much at the time as being, arguably, the most important experience of my life.

I cherish deeply the relationship I have always had with my kids. Through every stage of development, I have felt close to them. I loved them as toddlers and as teens. Today I consider them two of my best friends. Of all the things I have done in my life, I think I did being a dad the best. And I am absolutely certain I wouldn't have been as good a dad as I was had I not had the chance to baby sit for my little sister.

I am forever grateful for the opportunity my parents gave me.

And I deeply thank Joy for being such a good teacher.

Chapter Six

Now that I have survived what I have and arrived at this particular point in time, I would like to reflect on who I've become. Richard Bach suggests in *Running From Safety* that it isn't answers we seek, but *forever questions*—those questions that "asked again, bring you just the answers you need just the minute you need them." Questions like "Who am I?"

I remember a guidance unit I used to teach where I would ask a volunteer to come to the front of the room where I would then ask, "Who are you?"

"Joe Smith."

"Who," I'd repeat, "are you?"

"Bill Smith's son."

"But who are you?"

"I'm a fourteen-year-old boy."

"Who are you really?" I would continue asking ten or twelve times. Students struggled with this. You could feel the empathy from others in the room. Some got angry. But each answer revealed more than the previous one. After exhausting the factual data, they began to share interests or beliefs they held. That was the intent, to make students, and not just the one who now wished he hadn't volunteered, think about who they really were. Who they were deep inside.

To further prove the point, I would offer up a bio sheet about me. "I am Bob Cushman. I was born on October 16, 1935, in Minot, North Dakota. I graduated from high school in 1953. I am married and have two, three, or four children (depending on when this was and how you happen to count). I went to Minot State College and later graduated with a counseling degree from the University of North Dakota. I have a brother and a sister. My dad's name is Jack, and my mother's name is Lucylle. My middle name is Allen and I live at 633 Hudson Street in Paynesville, Minnesota. My phone number is 243-4687" . . . and about this time I'd wrap it up by adding, "and isn't that boring as hell."

They agreed.

And rightly so. There would follow a discussion on what makes a person interesting. Conclusions were predictable. Beliefs, interests, passions, experiences, and a lot of other non-factual things that really matter. Most of the time, we don't discover these things about people because it is safer to skim the surface than it is to get down to the bones. We are like Sgt. Joe Friday on *Dragnet*, "Just give me the facts ma'am."

As I read the question in Bach's book, it dawned on me I had only guided students through this exercise and never done it myself. That hardly seemed fair, so on March 27, 1996 (the specific date is important because, like any of us, I might come up with different answers on any other day), I set my trusty felt-tip to paper and I wrote:

"Who Am I ?"
> I am !!!
> I am a sage—a wise elder—a wisdom keeper.
> I am both saint and sinner—good and evil.
> I am a friend—it's what I do best.
> I am a husband.
> I am a father—and a damn good one
> I am a lover—in the purest sense of that word.

23

I am a survivor—of divorce, cancer, a heart attack, among other things.

I am the spiritual being I have been waiting to become.

I am a member of the fire-origin species.

I am becoming . . .

I am a storyteller; a teacher, writer, speaker.

I am a mentor.

I am funny (by whatever definition you give that word).

I am a golfer (not by all standards, but at least by my own)

I am passionate about what I believe.

I am a child of God.

I am a child.

I am a geezer.

I am creative.

I am special, wonderful, unique, lovable, and imperfect—and that's okay.

I am Cosmic Bob, the Sweet Baboo.

I am a St. Louis Cardinal fan—since 1946—so I guess that means I am loyal.

I am one-quarter Irish—the only part of my ethnicity which seems to matter.

I am human, whatever that means.

I am free to be me.

I am a wounded healer.

I am a lover of music.

I am a believer.

I am a leader.

I am silly.

I am a grandfather.

I am a lover of all good art.

I am happy.

I am loved.

I am serene—at least more so than ever before, so it seems like serenity.

I am a whole bunch.

I am easy-going and relatively easy to get along with.

I am a seeker.

I am nice.

"I yam what I yam, and tha's all I yam !"

I like this list. I like the fact that I didn't do much quantifying. I may or may not be all of these things in another's perspective. I may be more. Or less. On any given day, I would add or detract from this list. But this is the list I made that day in March. I am well-satisfied with it. I like who I am.

Who are you today?

Chapter Seven

I was born with non-convergent eyes. In 1940, an eye, nose, and throat doctor in Minot convinced my parents that, even though he had never performed the operation to correct crossed-eyes, he was competent and skilled enough to do it.

He was wrong.

When my parents took me home from the hospital, my left eye was still splayed left, and I had the additional problem that I could no longer see out of it. The doctor apparently cut a muscle he wasn't supposed to, or he nicked a nerve or something. He wasn't sure which. It's not entirely true to say that I can't see out of that eye . . . I can see a little bit. Actually the peripheral vision isn't too bad. But I am considered legally blind in my left eye. The cockeyed look led to endless teasing in grade school and didn't help my love life in high school either. I think I have adjusted and adapted quite well, and true friends are always able too see beneath the surface. It has never been a real problem. To avoid embarrassing classes, groups, and audiences, I always told them to "watch my right eye because it's always focused where I'm looking, and the left one wanders around and I don't know what the hell its looking at because I can't see out of it." That always worked to avoid those embarrassing "is he looking at me" glances around the room. It eased the tension. Gentle humor usually does. So the eye has never been more than a minor irritant and a cause, occasionally, for curiosity and idle conversation. I do have to admit that I have always feared losing the sight in my right eye, and the rest of you have no idea how terrifying it is to get a speck of dust in your right eye while surrounded by semis traveling eighty miles per hour on a freeway.

In 1987 I was involved in a Wellness Weekend for adults, on the Upper Peninsula of Michigan, near where Jimmy Stewart filmed *Anatomy of a Murder*. The UP is so beautiful. It's a shame more movies aren't filmed there. The theme for this particular weekend was masks. We paired up on Friday night to sculpt a mask on our partner's face. On Saturday night, materials were provided for each of us to decorate our individual masks, and at the closing ceremony on Sunday, we were to explain to the group why we chose our particular adornments. Great exercise.

My partner was Carroll Ann Swanson, a lady who worked as a chemical dependency counselor in the adolescent unit at Marquette General Hospital. We had never met prior to our mask-making, but it turned out the masks were an excellent foundation on which to build a relationship. Having a personal mask made of your face is a very warm experience. Strips of the treated gauze are dipped in warm water and lovingly molded to the contours of your face. It becomes a gentle face massage, and the result is a molded image of your visage. I wasn't to realize the accuracy of the likeness Carroll Ann created until Saturday night. She was a wonderful partner. I don't recall any of our conversation that night. I only remember the healing touch she applied to my face—and I, I hope, to hers. In addition to two masks, we created that night a bond that still exists in spite of the fact our paths rarely cross.

On Saturday night, we were supplied with all sorts of decorating materials. There were paints, beads, ribbons, feathers, crayons, bright pieces of cloth, sequins, stars, and a host of other craft stuff. There were no restrictions as to how we could use these treasures to adorn our now-hardened likenesses. We couldn't have had a more creative environment. Immediately the room was buzzing with dozens of folks scurrying around to snatch up items that caught his or her eye—or heart. Everyone was busy. It was very festive. Music was playing; people were sharing stories and laughing. Everyone seemed really caught up in the atmosphere.

Except me. I moved from table to table picking up various baubles and trinkets but I always replaced each one on its pile. My mind toyed with dozens of ideas as my fingers toyed with the trimmings. Nothing seemed right. I just couldn't get going. And I had no idea why. Every color I touched seemed wrong. So did every feather. Every bead. People asked me what was wrong, and I couldn't tell them. Finally it hit me. I wasn't finding a fit for anything because I knew I wasn't intended to decorate this particular mask. I needed Becky to complete this mask.

Becky is the foster daughter who was about to graduate and walk out of our lives. It wasn't what we wanted, but both Mary and I felt quite certain that when she drove away the day following her graduation, she was moving permanently. I knew that I needed to ask Becky to leave me a symbolic representation of our relationship. I knew how I felt, but I wasn't sure of her thoughts and feelings. I knew that what I had to do was bring this blank mask home and ask her to beautify it for me.

I wasn't sure if that would fit the occasion, so I approached Steve, our mask-making guide for the weekend, and explained my dilemma. Of course, he said yes and invited me to share with the group at Sunday's closing why my mask was still white while each of their's was ablaze with color and ornamentation. As he chatted, Steve kept studying my mask. Finally he asked if I had taken a close look at my mask. I told him I thought I had looked it over pretty carefully and and that was followed by a conversation something like this:

Steve asked, "Do you notice anything different or special about this mask?"

"No," I told him. "I do think Carroll Ann did a great job."

"I think it's exceptional," he agreed. "Look at it again."

I studied the mask closely before telling him, "I don't seem to be able to see what you want me to see. Help me out?"

"Look at the eyes," he offered.

I was still in a fog. "I don't see anything unusual."

"Are you sure?" he questioned.

"I'm sorry, Steve," I answered. "I just don't see anything out of the ordinary."

"The left eye, Bob. Look again at the way Carroll Ann did your left eye. The socket is more open on that side so that it gives the impression you are looking out of the side, just the way your real eye actually does." Once he explained what he saw, I was able to see it too. Sure enough. The left eye on the mask gave the appearance of gazing to the left. Carroll Ann had, without realizing it she was to tell me later, captured the true functioning of my left eye.

"That's amazing," I told Steve. "I don't know what to say."

"It is interesting that she picked up on it . She must have some strong intuitive vibes." And then he asked. "Do you know very much about non-convergent eyes?"

"Nothing," I confessed, "except what I've learned living with one all my life."

Steve went on to tell me that, as a student at Northern Michigan University, he was currently doing a research paper on non-convergent eyes. Talk about a serendipitous moment. Lends a little credence to the Buddhist precept "when the student is ready the teacher appears." He had become interested because of a relative with non-convergent eyes. As a matter of fact, he had some of his research in his car. He asked me to wait because there was a book he wanted to show me. He was back in a couple minutes with a few pamphlets and a large book. He gave me the pamphlets and then opened the book to two pages that had about forty or fifty pictures of men and women with non-convergent eyes.

There was considerable variety in the photos but, in addition to the eyes, there was one thing each had in common with the others. All these people were white. The caption at the bottom of the page explained that all of these folks were either in prison or in a mental hospital.

After letting this information soak in, Steve flipped to the next page which contained another forty or fifty pictures of different men and women with non-convergent eyes. The people in these photographs, however, were all people of color: Africans, Asians, Hispanics, East Indians, and Native Americans. And all were shamans, priests, medicine men/women, padres, or other spiritual leaders in their respective communities.

Cultures of color, it would seem, view non-convergent eyes as a spiritual gift—a way of looking at the world in a unique way that offers wisdom and enlightenment. White cultures, on the other hand, tend to see this same trait as a character flaw, the owner of which is not to be trusted and might even be feared. Self-fulfilling prophecy, being cross-cultural, explains the results.

My take is that neither position is wholly accurate. Non-convergent eyes are merely a characteristic like any other. Some people's eyes are blue while others are brown. Still others are green or hazel. Some people have large eyes, others small. Many are almond shaped, while others more round. Some are non-convergent while others look straight ahead. None of this has any bearing on what kind of person the bearer is. But I do have to confess that what Steve shared with me that night made me feel just a little bit better about myself.

When Becky finished decorating the mask, she explained her work to me, and her explanation had none of the white culture interpretation and a whole lot of the people's-of-color views. That made me feel really good.

Chapter Eight

I always wanted to write poetry. I love poems. I love the sounds of poetry. I love the imagery and alliteration. I love the carefully chosen words. Poetry seems like it's better, somehow, than prose—more pure. But I know nothing about poetry. I know nothing of iambic pentameter or haiku. I know none of the rules. But I go ahead and write poetry anyway. My poems have wound up in some of the finest wastebaskets and some of the worst looking dumpsters in about thirty different states and three or four provinces. My rules for writing poetry are to make the lines uneven and try to write from my soul. That said, here is the one poem I have written that I have small amount of pride in:

My Sacred Space
There is a place in the universe
that belongs to me.
I didn't buy it.
It was given me.
It is my birthright.
Just because I am here,
because I am a child of God,

31

Time Flies Whether You're Having Fun or Not

I have been given a piece of the universe
that is all mine.
I can't tell anyone where it is
as that would give away
more than I choose to give.
I can, however, share
bits and pieces
with whoever I choose to trust.
I can choose to share some of the
colors, shapes, and sounds—
Some of the magic
of my gift—my secret place.
All I ask in return is that
you treat my secret place
with gentleness,
with respect,
and with love.
After all,
it is sacred.

Chapter Nine

Sometimes I think my life has just sort of happened. Oh, I've made my share of lists and plans, but those have mostly got me through the day or from one week to the next. The really big stuff has never resulted from long-range planning. It has pretty much fallen into place by dumb luck or divine intervention. Perhaps a little of each.

I'll fast forward through my developmental years. Suffice it to say I made more than my share of dumb decisions, and I arrived at high school graduation a very irresponsible person certain of only one thing—I never wanted to set foot in a school again. I cruised through the summer of 1953 dispatching cabs for my dad and partying. It wasn't costing me anything to live at home, and the meager wages kept me in cigarettes and beer. Life couldn't have suited me better.

Until August. That's when Dad asked me what I planned to do in the fall. Of course, I told him the status quo suited me just fine. He said, "Okay. But now that you are out of school, I'll have to start charging you room and board."

"I can't afford room and board on what I'm making," I explained.

Of course he knew that. He made a counter offer. "I'll let you stay at home for nothing if you go to college."

College? Three months earlier I had vowed never to set foot in a school again, and now my dad was offering me a chance to go to college. Was he out of his mind? Did he not remember that I had been suspended from high school? Twice! This was his son, Bob, he was talking to. On the other hand, I could continue living at home and not have to look for a real job.

I loved college. I loved cutting classes to play cards in the student union. I loved the parties. I loved going to football and basketball games. I loved all the new girls I was meeting. What I wasn't too crazy about was going to class and studying. My first quarter grades were four Ds and an F. I actually flunked Freshman Orientation. This was a silly course about how to brush your teeth, comb your hair, and why you should wear deodorant. The freshman class was loaded with vets returning from Korea, and we had this required class about personal hygiene. I never went back after the first day.

Those first quarter grades earned me academic probation.

I was smart enough, however, to know that if I worked just hard enough to maintain a C average, I could stay in school and continue my lifestyle. I lived at home, worked a little at the cab office and began working at a local radio station as a late-night disc jockey. Life was sweet. I joined a fraternity and became even more of a professional student. I cruised that way for three years.

Two things interrupted my senior year. Not that it mattered academically. I didn't have enough credits to have graduated anyway. In January my girlfriend became pregnant, and I quit school to get married and pursue a full-time radio career. I got a job at KSJB in Jamestown, North Dakota, but we didn't like the town or the job. By August, going back to school seemed better than staying where we were. I made an appointment with the Dean of Men and when he asked me what I wanted to major in, I asked, "What's the quickest way out of here?"

34

That's how I became a social studies teacher.

Becoming a husband and father are part of that last paragraph, too, and there is no question I was meant to be a father or that I belonged in education. Perhaps my wives have had doubts at times about the husband part. My first wife did for sure.

I started teaching in Cavalier, North Dakota, where I stayed for six years. During that time, I turned down a radio announcing job and an offer to teach in a larger school in the western part of the state. Starting something new seemed such a pain. The fact that I stayed in Cavalier is significant to the next turn of events because of its proximity to Grand Forks and the University of North Dakota. One Saturday, we were shopping in Grand Forks, and I bumped into an old college friend, Bob McIlroy. I asked him what he was doing, and he answered, "I'm studying to become a high school counselor."

And I swear I responded, "What the hell is a counselor?"

He explained what counseling was. I had been a little dissatisfied with teaching, and this sounded perfect for me. I picked Bob's brain for every scrap of information he had about it. By the end of the week, I had found out the university would be teaching "Introduction to Counseling" off-campus in Cavalier the next fall. I enrolled in that and a follow-up course winter quarter. By spring, I'd quit my job and enrolled in the Counseling and Guidance Institute at the university.

Thus, a counseling career fell into my lap. How I wound up in Paynesville, Minnesota, was not a conscious choice either. We had wanted to go into southern Minnesota, and I was scheduled to interview in Waterville. But in the spring of 1965, flood waters were so high we couldn't cross the river to that part of the state. I still see signs nailed on trees pointing out those high water marks when I drive through some southern suburbs of Minneapolis. So I took the only job offer I had north of the Minnesota River—Paynesville. I've never regretted that twist of fate either.

Twice we did consider moving. The first was shortly before the end of my second year here. A friend who was teaching at the University of Connecticut called to tell me I could have a job in their Family Life Education Department. On his recommendation, the department head was willing to hire me sight unseen. All I had to do was say yes. I had three days to give him an answer. We were living in an apartment at the time and had a chance to move into a house across the street. So our decision was to either move across the street or across the country. I didn't think I'd given being a counselor much of a chance. We stayed. That determined the next ten or twelve years. The kids grew up here, which they cherish, and life was pretty good to all of us. We were happy. At least I was happy. My wife was maybe not so happy. She decided we shouldn't be married any longer. I didn't agree, but it turned out she was right.

I found myself alone, but felt I should stay in Paynesville for one year. I thought it important my son, Mark, who was in his first year of college, should have that stability for at least a year. But I vowed I definitely needed to get away from everything and start over when that year was up.

One year.

I'm still here. Things just kept happening. About a month after my wife, Mary, said she didn't want a second date, we found ourselves at the same restaurant where we started talking. One thing led to another, and we've been together over twenty years. We've watched her son, Troy, grow to manhood and get married. Our foster daughter, Becky, was "left on our doorstep" in 1983 so we made her part of the family. She gave us a grandson, Jordan. In 1982 I got involved doing workshops, seminars, and facilitating groups at weekend retreats called PIPfests. In 1993 the state legislature created a window of opportunity for retirement that I leaped through pretty much without thinking.

You may have noticed throughout this entire narrative I have only been adamant about two decisions. One was that I'd never set foot in a school after high school and the second was to leave Paynesville following the divorce. I don't encourage others to follow my lead in planning their lives, but I'm glad I didn't leave the big decisions up to someone who thinks like I do.

Chapter Ten

My Grandpa Perry was Irish, and my Grandpa Cushman English. My grandmothers, Swedish and Norwegian, respectively. Given the historical hostility between the Irish and English and the disdain the two Scandinavian countries held for one another, I was genetically programmed to have an inner civil war going on constantly. Add the facts that I grew up with a blue collar mentality—work hard, play hard, sin hard, and pray hard—in a tough Midwest railroad town and that alcohol ran like sap in my family tree, and you'd hardly expect a happy childhood.

And you would be right. But in spite of the pain and anxiety, I find myself looking back with great amounts of nostalgia at certain aspects of childhood—that wonderful time when all I had to do was go to school and take an occasional bath. These memories are less about people and more about place. What I truly find myself longing for are the places of my youth. To be sure, these places were filled with people, but it is the places themselves that stick in my mind more than the names and faces. Except Anita Valor. She was really cute, and I had a huge crush on her.

I barely remember the house I lived in for the first eight years. I know there was a porch that went around the front and the north side and that it was next door to a church, the steeple of which was home to a vast air force of bats. That's about it. It's almost like my life didn't begin to take form until we moved to 314 Ninth Street, N.W. That neighborhood is indelibly printed in my mind. Liebergs lived two doors down from us, and they had converted their garage into a small grocery store. An awful lot of my nickels went for pop, candy, and fudgesicles in that store. Gallos lived between the store and us, and Organs lived on the north side. I think Mrs. Organ was probably the sweetest little old lady I've ever known. At least until my mom started to age. McCormicks lived just down the alley, and Uglums lived behind us on Eighth Street. Hansons, with their many children, lived across the street on Fourth Avenue, and Valors across from them. Later, Kay Davidson moved on the corner of Third Avenue, and she almost made me forget about Anita. Blaisdells lived a block south on Ninth Street.

The neighborhood was beautiful with scores of large trees, dozens of manicured green lawns, and thousands of flowers. Every backyard held a burst of color in their endless variety of flowers and flowered vines. Everybody knew everybody else. And all us kids played together. Kids from blocks away came to play in our neighborhood. Every summer night there was a street game of some sort. The most popular was "Who'll Draw the Frying Pan," a local version of hide-and-seek. And every day there was a pick-up game of baseball on Fourth Avenue, between Eighth and Ninth Streets. Home plate was a piece of cardboard in the middle of the street, as was second base. First and third were trees on the boulevards. Games could last for hours with only brief interruptions to let cars pass through.

Our football field was Ninth Street, either right in front of our house or a block south by Blaisdells. There were several basketball courts wherever dads had nailed backboards to garage roofs. McCormick's was one of the better "courts." We had a basket, too, but our side porch cut into the width of the driveway and made it pretty hard to have games. It was great for a little one-on-one or games of horse or twenty-one. In those days, there was very little overlap in professional seasons, and kids usually played whatever sport was in season.

Winters were for sledding and tobogganing on north hill and skating at Bissell's skating rink, where you could skate down the riverbank to the river, which was about ten feet lower. I remember a lot of games of crack-the-whip on that river. Late spring was the time for the Indianapolis 500. For about two weeks, we got on our bikes and held our own Indy right there on Ninth Street. Ron Lindlauf, Dennis Crites, Marv Thornby, and I staked out an oval that started in front of my house went to the northernmost driveway on that side of the street across to the opposing driveway, down the straightaway to Davidson's driveway, across to Lieberg's and down that straightaway past my house again. The number of laps was always predetermined. The turns were sharp, and there were a lot of skinned knees and elbows, but it was a great time. Ron always won.

The woods behind the houses on Fourth Avenue provided a wonderful venue for "cowboys and Indians," one of the more popular games for guys in our area. War games were big too. Those same woods served as battlefields. Many of us had dads, brothers, cousins, and/or uncles fighting in World War II, and playing war seemed patriotic and supportive. Most kids had cap pistols or homemade guns that shot rubber bands. I also liked going over to my cousin Dick's house to play either cowboys and Indians or war. Minot sits in a valley and at that time the hills behind his place were uninhabited. Those hills were pretty barren and looked for all the world like the same ones Hopalong Cassidy or ReoRyder rode over on their way to save the wagon train in the movies. There were a few small caves that took little imagination to turn into enemy hideouts or pill boxes, whichever was needed on a particular day. North hill was to become a place memory for my teen years, too. That's where we would park our cars and listen to Harry Caray on KMOX, the voice of St. Louis, as he broadcast the Cardinal games.

There were two places from my past dubbed "the hole." The first was a place on the Mouse River, which winds its way throughout the town. Along the riverbank that abutted Tenth Street, about three blocks from my house, was a niche that God had carved out that made the most wonderful swimmin' hole of His whole swimmin' hole designing career. About a dozen feet below street level was this little "beach" about thirty feet wide and twenty feet deep cut into the side of the riverbank. Steps had been dug into the embankment to provide easy access to the lower level and, thus, to the water that was forty to fifty yards wide at that point—and probably somewhere near fifteen to twenty feet deep. On the east rim of this little dug-out area was a huge oak tree that stretched out about half-way across the river. Standing at the top—street level—you could grab the knotted end of the rope tied to the oak and swing out over the water, letting loose at the height of your arc and dropping into the middle of the river. With a little practice you could learn to dive from the rope. It was the single most fun thing I can remember doing as a child. To the boys of that neighborhood, it was far more popular than the municipal pool in Roosevelt Park. Maybe skinny dipping had something to do with that. I know it had something to do with the boys-only nature of "the hole."

The other hole was Selk's pool hall on Main Street beneath the Orpheum Theater. This was the hangout for Minot High School boys. There were six public grade schools when I grew up, but students from all six filtered uptown to Minot Junior High School. At four o'clock after the last bell of the day, about a quarter of the male population could be seen traveling the five and one-half blocks to what we affectionately, almost reverently, called "the hole." For my gang, this was command headquarters. All activity flowed from that hallowed, smoke-filled room at the bottom of the stairs on North Main. If we were planning a movie, we met at the hole. If the plan for the evening was a poker game or a night at the Fifty-Two Club, we met at the hole first. If you had no plans, you went to the hole and stayed there. Everything started there. It was the place to be. Some of my dearest high school friendships began down there. It was where my horizons began to expand.

I've saved my cousin's driveway for last because it is such a unique memory.There is much that is hard to imagine—or describe—unless you were part of that time. And that place. World War II was being waged across the seas, but it became our war too. This war seemed to consume all Americans. It was practically all adults talked about. At every movie, we saw newsreels that kept us posted as to what was happening in Italy, Germany, North Africa, or the Pacific. Even our cartoons were filled with caricatures of Hitler, Hirohito, and Mussolini. Often, before the movie started, someone would come onstage to sell war bonds. At school, we were urged to buy stamps that we placed in books redeemable for war bonds. Victory gardens popped up in nearly every yard. We collected scrap metal that could be turned into bullets and bombs. We limited our use, through rationing, of any and every material that was needed for the war effort. In short, we all were literally a part of the fight. Every mother's son of us, from three to eighty-three, did his part to bring down the Axis Powers.

Dick's older brother, Don, was in the army, and I had a couple other cousins in the service, too. It is only natural that war was part of our play. With large numbers, it was relatively easy to make up ways to play war. When there were only two, you had to be more creative. Dick and I spent a lot of time together, just the two of us. Neither of us could afford to buy the factory-made soldiers at Woolworth's. We had to improvise. And we were quite good at it. Sticks of all kinds served as soldiers, and his driveway became our battle zone. Ammunition was the tiny rocks abundant in that driveway. (It wasn't paved.) We laid out elaborate battlefields. Our stick men were deployed strategically. Sometimes the battle plan called for armies to move forward en masse but it was more common to send small detachments to outflank the enemy.

Matchboxes and other small receptacles were utilized as

jeeps, tanks, and planes. Larger sticks worked as cannons, and bigger stones made fine grenades, mortars, and bombs. If a grenade or mortar shell hit a foxhole or bunker you had to break the sticks therein to indicate those men were dead. We sometimes had battles that lasted all afternoon. I found that I could entertain myself with this game, too. When I look back on this experience, I am stunned by the ingenuity and creativity we displayed. Our ability to make-do and create our own fun was incredible. I can't help but feel a little sad when I see kids at play today. I know they are missing something I cherish from my childhood.

I don't go back to Minot very much. My brother, Jack, still lives there, and that's the only strong connection I have left. When I do go back, the only thing still remaining is the house on Ninth Street, but that's just four walls and a roof now. The pool hall is gone. So is the swimming hole. I'm not sure I could even find Dick's old house, and north hill is filled with houses. The neighborhood looks much the same. The trees are even bigger and more beautiful. The lawns are still green and nicely trimmed. And there's still a lot of flowers. But there's no one playing ball in the streets. So everything I cherish is gone. But I know where it is.

It's inside me.

> "O, Great Spirit,
> who made all races,
> look kindly upon the
> whole human family
> and take away the
> arrogance and hatred
> which separates us
> from our brothers."
> —Cherokee prayer

Chapter Eleven

I just don't understand racism—or any of the other "isms," for that matter. And I don't understand all of racism's relatives like prejudice, bigotry, discrimination, and segregation. I simply, flat-out do not understand how one person can feel (s)he is better than someone else, for any reason. And I don't even understand why I don't understand. I've been surrounded by it my whole life. On the other hand, something seems to have protected me from it—sort of immunized me, as it were.

I'm not saying I don't have my biases and opinions. I certainly have my share. I've always been a pretty opinionated person, and, in my dotage, it seems to be getting worse. But I think my opinions about people are based on attitudes and behaviors, not on the color of skin or some other fact about who they are. There are a lot of behaviors I'm not overly fond of. I don't like rudeness whether its coming from someone cutting me off in traffic or interrupting me when I'm talking. And I think there are a lot of really stupid, to me, things people do that bug me. But I do stupid and rude things, too. We're all pretty much the same in that regard. It has nothing to do with skin color, ethnic background, or cultural values. Folks are folks.

And that's why I don't understand prejudice.

Minot, where I grew up, was pretty much a white-minded community; people tended to see things dualistically: right or wrong, farm or city, black or white, Democrat or Republican. But the town included a pretty good mix of people. The majority were of Northern European extraction, but there were decent numbers of Asian, Greek, Jewish, Black, and Native American folks. I had friends in all groups. So when I heard the slurs and effronteries aimed at any group I didn't understand.

I heard all the hateful insults and innuendoes. I abhor the labels people use to describe others. I think they are the most obscene words in our language. Natives were so often referred to as "lazy drunks" and "savages." And I heard "dumb nigger" used to describe the Blacks. Jewish folks were "tightwads who would cheat you out of every nickel you had." Asians were "sneaky," and the Greeks were "dirty." I heard these comments from Dad's cabdrivers, and from their customers. I heard them from railroad workers and farmers. I heard them from prominent businessmen. I heard them from policemen when I went to the station to visit my aunt who was the town police matron. You could hear these comments at the Country Club or the pool hall. But mostly I heard these comments from kids at school.

But I could never figure it out. None of it fit my experience. Bob Swamura and Larry Nagatomo were two of my very best childhood friends. Up until I moved out of his neighborhood, I spent more time at Larry's house than I did at my own. I liked him. I liked his family. I didn't see anything sneaky about any of them. I liked the Maragos boys. My uncle worked in their dad's grocery store, and there was nothing dirty about it. We bought a lot of groceries there so we must have felt it was a clean enough place. And the cab drivers' favorite coffee shop was run by a Greek family. We ate there. It must not have been too dirty either. As a teen I bought a lot of my clothes at a men's clothing shop run by a Jewish family. The weren't trying to cheat me out of anything. Their daughter, Janet, and I were good friends who shared a lot of confidences. She was a very generous person. I had a crush on Shelley Strauss, another Jewish girl in my class, when I was in tenth grade. Her dad ran a jewelry store on Main Street. I bought my first wife's wedding ring from him. All the Black people treated me very nicely. Many of them were customers of the cab company, and they knew me from the time I was a toddler.

And that's why I don't get it. I certainly wasn't the only one in Minot, or any place else on the planet, who had friends who came from diverse backgrounds. I wasn't the only one doing business with them. Everybody did. All the people who were saying the hateful things were also eating in Greek and Chinese restaurants and buying their groceries in Greek-run stores. We all purchased our goods and services from people whose families did not come from Northern Europe. We worked side by side. We sat next to each other in the theater or at school. We played together. On many a Sunday, Dad and I went to Minot Mallards baseball games and sat in the first-base bleachers with Saul Davis and some of the other Black businessmen from town.

So what was the prejudice about? Where did it come from? That's what I don't get. There was nothing in my experience that would indicate we weren't just all friends and neighbors working together and living together in relative harmony. Instead there existed some kind of undercurrent that said we were supposed to harbor this bigotry— some kind of legacy. It had to have passed on from generation to generation like other myths—such as Paul Bunyan and Robin Hood, for example. And it had even less credibility. In a way we were like Dick Gregory, the Black comedian-turned-activist, who described the difference between the attitudes of Southerners and Northerners concerning Black people. "In the South," Gregory observed, "they like us, but they don't love us. Up North they love us, but they don't like us."

The people of my upbringing, in their naivete, got it backwards. We liked the folks from the different cultures—we truly did—but we apparently didn't love them. They didn't know why; they had just been taught that way. Some of the true colors began to show when the Minot Air Base came into existence in the sixties. Over half the population there was made up of people of color. Many of the personnel began seeking off-base housing. This, of course, meant many black families were seeking to move to previously all-white neighborhoods. And the biases that had been lying dormant for so many years began to surface.

I'll never forget the day I learned this truth about my dad. I had always considered him to be about as free from prejudice as any person I knew. One summer I came home to work for him. (I always needed a summer job to augment the pittance I got teaching in North Dakota.) Dad was sitting in the living room when I walked in the door. I commented on the fact that he hadn't sold the house he owned next door. He told me he had a couple of good offers, but he couldn't sell to them because they were black families from the air base. He proceeded to hand me all the twisted logic that has been used all over the country for generations to "keep the coloreds in their place."

I couldn't believe I was hearing this from my dad. I was immediately incensed, and an argument followed where we both said things we later regretted. Neither, of course, convinced the other, and we both stormed off to pout. Later that night I went for a long walk, and I remember crying my eyes out as I walked. For the first time in twenty-five years, I had to face the fact that prejudice was part of, not just my community history, but my family history as well. It too had to have been there all along. Why hadn't I seen it? I didn't understand then. I don't now. I just don't get it.

What I really don't get is that, in spite of all the efforts of so many, there seems to be as much hatred and racism as there ever was. My entire adult life has been rampant with good people working diligently to improve race relations. And we've made no real headway. Oh, we've passed laws and established commissions to study the issue and set up programs like Affirmative Action to level the playing field a little. None of this seems to have much impact where it really matters—in the hearts of the people. Some hearts seem to have even hardened as a result of these efforts.

I don't have any solution. You can't solve what you don't understand. I do suspect there is a strong connection between the names we call people and how we treat them. When you refer to an individual by a label, be it Spic, Yid, Nigger, Whitey, or whatever, you give yourself permission to treat that person as a thing, as something less than human. I observed that in schools for thirty-five years. The kids, who are called names, given labels, are mistreated by those who call them the names. I think the labels have got to go before we're going to see any change of heart. A professor I had in graduate school made a statement in class one day in 1964 that I can't forget. I've debated the merits of this statement many times. Try as I might I can't convince myself he was wrong. He said to the class. "We have to reach a point where we can say, 'I hate Jackie Robinson,' rather than 'I hate that black #@*$.'" He chose Jackie Robinson, I'm sure because of who he was and his stature in the black community. In today's world, he would have chosen Michael Jordan or Tiger Woods. His inference is simple: we need to make our decisions about people based on who they are as individuals, not on some extraneous fact about them.

The same logic would apply if you were to say, I hate John F. Kennedy rather than I hate that white *%@*-#. Color is a fact, not a value. We all choose who we will like or dislike based on interests, attitudes, beliefs, and other commonalities. There's nothing wrong with that. Those should be the only criteria. Bessie Delany, one of the two centenarian black sisters who co-authored the best-selling book, *Having Our Say*, wrote simply, "All I ever wanted in my life was to be treated as an individual." Isn't that true for all of us? I don't think we can achieve that for any of us unless we can look past skin color, church affiliation, group membership, or ethnicity.

And, for God's sake, get rid of the labels. It just might help.

Chapter Twelve

I learned a lot from my children. I probably would have learned a lot more if I had been paying better attention. But like most young parents, I believed that I was the teacher, and they were supposed to learn from me. I was supposed to be doling out the wisdom—in huge doses. I think I'm doing a better job with my grandchildren. I hope so.

I went to graduate school as part of a federally promoted program designed to place guidance counselors in every school in the United States. To accomplish this, guidance institutes were established in several colleges and universities throughout the country. I was accepted to such an institute at the University of North Dakota in 1964. There were thirty of us in this particular institute. Those of us so institutionalized represented several states: Texas, Kansas, New York, Nebraska, Montana, Oregon, and Massachusetts, as well as the Dakotas and Minnesota. That was pretty much the extent of our diversity. We were all teachers, all male—and all white, except for Wayman Webster, an African-American from Texas.

We all liked Wayman, and it was, I think, mutual. Wayman's family stayed in Texas. Horror stories of North

Dakota winters shaped his wife's decision to enjoy the warmth of Texas. For several winters, I experienced the icy winds and bitter cold that plague the Red River Valley in January. I also spent one week in Texas in January. Believe me, the lady made a wise choice. Wayman spent the entire school year living apart from his family. He was the only member of our group in that situation.

As a group, we did a lot of socializing. Most of our families lived in close proximity in student housing units on campus. It was common to invite another couple or two over for coffee in the evening. Some studied at the library together. Nearly all of us paired off or grouped up to cram for exams. Many of us went to a local pub after classes every Friday for a few beers. We entered a team in the intramural basketball league (and, despite our advanced ages, almost won the championship). Some of us played handball or threw frisbees around the park. We went to plays and sporting events together. All thirty of us were in every class together. We became pretty tight.

Many of us, assuming Wayman was both lonely, so far from his family, and starved for home cooking, would invite him over for an evening meal. I only invited him once. Jodi was seven at the time and Mark five. I thought I needed to teach them something about what was about to take place. I didn't trust their natural instincts. Had I done nothing and said nothing, the evening would have passed without incident. Mark and Jodi would have been just fine had I left them alone.

But I wasn't that smart.

At some point prior to Wayman's arrival, it occurred to me that the kids had grown up in a lily-white world and had never seen nor talked with a black person. I knew they wouldn't do or say anything cruel, but I was afraid they might inadvertently make him feel self-conscious. Perhaps it was the embarrassment and anger I often felt around my dad's prejudices and racial slurs. Perhaps it was my own ignorance. Whatever. I plunged ahead with my plan. With my ego fully intact and my self-proclaimed wisdom in hand, I sat down with them to explain.

I started with the obvious. "The man who is coming to dinner is a Negro." (Remember, this was 1964.)

Jodi and Mark just looked at me with that "what's your point" look kids reserve for their parents when parents ramble cluelessly.

Missing this cue completely, I went on. "I know you've never seen a Negro before, and I don't want you to stare at him or ask him about his skin or hair. I don't want you to say anything that will make him feel different. Do you understand? (As I tell this story, I can't believe how stupid I was or how little faith I had in my kids.)

They stared at me. They looked at each other. They nodded.

"I'm counting on you guys . . ." and I blathered on to make sure they got the point. Finally satisfied that my wonderful parenting was complete for the moment, I sent them off to play until dinner was ready. They were, I'm sure, glad to escape the lecture chamber. They scampered off, and I smugly informed my wife that I had prepared the children for the evening. Geez! I could have been writing sitcoms back in the sixties. My real life lectures were as dumb as any ever delivered by Jim Anderson or Ward Cleaver.

The evening went smoothly. We had a drink and visited for a while before dinner. Kris served a nice family meal. The conversation was light and pleasant. Jodi and Mark were well-behaved, and everyone seemed to be having a nice time. My ducks were all in a row, and the evening was a success. Kris served vanilla ice cream for dessert.

Mark asked, "Can I have some chocolate syrup?"

Jodi's eyes widened. In her very best Lucy Van Pelt imitation, she admonished her little brother, "Don't say chocolate."

Silence.

Then laughter. Gales of laughter.

I had overplayed my hand. Big time. I don't remember the rest of the evening. I have felt bad about this event for thirty-five years. I know it was all ignorant innocence, but I feel I set my kids up. And I let them down. Maybe not quite as much as I felt my dad let me down, but I disappointed them just the same. And they probably didn't even realize it. I know Wayman laughed it off good-naturedly and probably hasn't given it a thought since.

But I have, and this is about me. Mark had merely asked a simple question. Jodi simply reflected what she learned from her dad a few hours earlier. The only one who behaved badly that evening was me. And it cost me. I was too embarrassed to ask Wayman back again. I didn't get to enjoy his company as much as I could have the rest of the year. We always pay a pretty steep price for our ignorance. I know I sure have.

I certainly learned a better lesson from my kids that night than they got from me.

Chapter Thirteen

When Mark was between his sophomore and junior years in high school, he had the best paying job of any four-teen-year old I've ever run across. It was for only half an hour, but he was paid most handsomely for that thirty min-utes. Most handsomely. In relating this, I have to confess my memory is a little fuzzy about some of the specifics, so when I say, for example, $4.00, it may not have been $4.00 at all. It may have actually been $3.50, or $4.10, or whatev-er. I really don't know. I suppose, if accurate detail were important to the story, I would do some research and obtain some facts. I'm quite lazy actually and accuracy is totally unnecessary for the story, so I didn't bother to check that sort of thing. So, with apologies to all anal-retentive readers, I shall continue,

The incident took place in 1975. Mark was hired for one of those government-sponsored youth-work programs that were popular at the time. Mark's job was an assistant to the custodial staff at the Paynesville Community Hospital. He was paid (wink, wink, nudge, nudge*) $4.00 an hour, and the program had a limit of (wink, wink, nudge, nudge) 280

*for all Monty Python fans

52

hours each participant was allowed to put in. The hours were to be completed within a ten-week period. By about the second or third Thursday in August, Mark had completed (w, w, n, n) 276 hours. He had four hours (accurate figure, by the way—my memory's not totally shot) to complete and was scheduled to work from 8:00 A.M. until noon on Friday (also accurate). At 11:30 A.M., he was mopping floors in one of the corridors. A large fan was positioned in the corridor to dry the floor quickly. At some point in carrying out his appointed task, he found it necessary to move the fan.

There may have been some carelessness involved, I really don't know, not having been there. As Mark reached for the fan, the little finger of his right hand came in close proximity to the whirling blade. In the battle that followed between blade and finger, the blade won. (It is very important for me to inform you that the personnel of the hospital at that time were totally different from the current staff and administration and the level of service was somewhat below what the citizens of this area now enjoy.) Mark could not find anyone to help him, so he walked the two blocks home. He showed the finger to his mom and me and told us he thought it might be broken. Since the pinky was dangling limply somewhere near his wrist we agreed.

I took him back to the hospital to get the finger set. There were no doctors to be found, so a nurse advised us to go to the clinic. The waiting room was filled, and, since we hadn't known in advance this would happen, we hadn't made an appointment. Somewhere between three and four o'clock that afternoon we finally saw a doctor who set the bone, cast the finger, and sent us on our merry way. So far two lessons had been learned. The first, of course, was that it is not a good idea to put your hand inside the protective wiring around an operating fan. The second lesson was that, if you were going to violate the first lesson, this particular hospital was not a good place to do it.

I want to recap here. At the time of the accident, Mark had one-half hour left to work for the summer. The ten-week period was up. The 280 hours were up. The program for which he was hired was completed. Totally over. There was no more program. This thirty minutes is, and I'm sure you are way ahead of me here, the half hour I mentioned in the first paragraph. Oh, I forgot to mention one more important thing. The doctor had told us the cast would have to be on six to eight weeks.

Two weeks later Mark got a check in the mail for over $200. The check was from an insurance company representing Minnesota Workman's Compensation. The hospital had been required by law to report the accident, and this payment, an accompanying letter explained, was for wages lost for this two-week period in which he couldn't work because of his injury. Mark was ecstatic. He had been planning to buy himself a good drum set. This meant he could upgrade. We explained he couldn't cash the check. There had to be some mistake. He wouldn't have worked those two weeks anyway; the program was over. I called a bookkeeper at the hospital, and she gave me the name of the local insurance agent to contact. I went to his office and carefully explained the situation, making sure he understood that Mark had only half an hour left to work. He agreed completely that Mark was not entitled to the money and told us not to cash the check. He sent a letter to the the parent company apprising them of the situation.

A week passed. Another week. Another check. I called the local agent. He called the parent company. He called me back. "Cash the checks," he told us, "the money legally belongs to Mark."

I protested. "This can't possibly be right. So far Mark has been paid over $400 for what was to have been thirty minutes work. At best, he should have got a couple bucks."

He spelled out for me the offical rules of Workman's Compensation. Roughly translated, his interpretaton was that a worker, when injured, shall receive payment for his normal work week until such a time as a doctor deems him fit to return to work. In Mark's case that would be when the cast was removed. I told him that might be another month. "Besides," I explained, "Mark is back in school. Surely they recognize he would no longer be working twenty-eight hours a week."

He laughed and told me to quit being an idiot. "Let Mark enjoy the money. Let him get a drum set." I begged him to make at least one more phone call to be absolutely certain we were to keep this windfall. He did so and was told the red tape involved in amending this would cost more than the money being paid Mark. They would not take the money back. They could not take the money back. It was Mark's money, and that was all there was to it. We gave up.

Mark got a third check covering two weeks. The doctor took the cast off after the seventh week, and Mark got one last check covering his final "week at work." When it was over, he had been paid approximately $780 for that half hour. That works out to an hourly pay rate of $1,560. That is a mighty handsome rate of pay for a fourteen-year-old custodial aide. He did buy himself a good drum set and has played professionally since his senior year of high school. He's been in bands in Minnesota, Colorado, and New York. He's played in Canada and Sweden.

I still can't help but feel there was something very wrong in how this incident was handled. It certainly was a nice break for Mark. It was an impetus to pursue drumming professionally. To a fourteen-year-old boy getting nearly $800 for nothing is like a sign there really is a God. I know Mark was and is grateful for the largess, and so am I. It may have been legal, but it just wasn't right. I don't know what would happen in similar circumstances today. I hope a glitch of this nature has been worked out. But we are dealing with the government here—two of them actually, federal and state. And I can't help but feel that when there is a conflict between two government agencies you can count on lunacy prevailing.

Chapter Fourteen

Sometime when you have nothing else to do try calculating the odds on this one. When I first came to Paynesville in 1965, one of my colleagues on the high school faculty was Henry Southworth. Put that in your memory bank. You will need it later.

Twelve generations ago, my great-great-whatever-grandfather, Robert Cushman, was a rather distinguished and well-to-do businessman in England. He was to become the chief financier of the *Mayflower*. Really! Robert was living in London around 1609 and, like many other businessmen of the day, was rather unhappy with certain government policies, i.e. taxes, state religion—that sort of thing. He joined the Separatists, a band of dissidents who fled to Holland because King James wasn't overly fond of most businessmen either. These dissenters were determined to establish a colony in the New World, and Robert was delegated to negotiate passage to a proposed colony in Virginia. After years of failure, futility, and frustration, a patent was finally obtained from the good king, along with permission to enjoy freedom of religion in the New World.

In 1920, 102 passengers boarded the *Mayflower* and set sail for the unknown across the sea. Robert wasn't among them. You know most of that story, so I'll stick with what you don't. I personally have always admired Robert's wisdom in staying behind, apparently waiting to make sure they made it. Remember, nearly half of them died that first winter, while he slept comfortably in his warm bed and ate regular meals with which he was familiar. I can picture myself making that same decision: "That's okay. You guys go ahead. I'll catch up with you later. Have a nice trip."

He did come over the next year, sailing on the *Fortune.* His son Thomas came with him. Robert stayed only a short time as business called him back to England. He left Thomas in the care of Governor William Bradford in Massachusetts. This is the same William Bradford who governed the colony for about thirty years, probably helped write the *Mayflower Compact,* and is credited with organizing the first Thanksgiving. (Side bar: Thomas was to become a famous minister in the colonies, and he married Mary Allerton, who is sometimes a footnote in history books. She was to become the last surviving member of those who sailed on the *Mayflower,* living until 1699. Really!)

To tell you the truth I have never been very excited about coming from this background. I know being a *Mayflower* descendant is a big deal for a lot of folks, but I've pretty much considered it merely an accident of birth. I don't deny my ancestry, but this particular item just isn't a big deal to me. I figure the gene pool had become pretty diluted after twelve generations. Others in my family see it otherwise. Consequently, I do own a genealogy compiled by a Herbert Cushman, a distant cousin of my dad, back in 1944. Everybody in my family of origin got one, but I've never talked much about it. It just gathers dust in a bookshelf. It's doubtful anyone in Paynesville, other than my wife and kids, even knew about it.

Until March 16, 1972. On that date Lanny Lundquist, then editor of *The Paynesville Press,* wrote his weekly column about my lineage. I can't remember exactly how Lanny got the story but I remember it being related to this turn of events: Don Torbenson, Superintendent of Schools, and his wife, Gladys, had taken a trip to New England. One of their stops was Old Burial Hill in Plymouth where Don was quite surprised to find the most conspicuous object on the hill was a twenty-five-foot-high granite column known as the Cushman Monument. It was erected in memory of both Robert and Thomas Cushman, the latter being buried there. I've never seen it, but I accept Don's description as a "very impressive sight." He brought me a souvenir booklet that describes all the gravesites, and we spent a pleasant hour or so with him as he told me of his trip and I filled him in on the little I knew of my ancestry.

Somehow Lanny learned of the story and wrote his column. Okay, now it's time to pull Henry Southworth from your memory bank. Remember you stored him there in the first paragraph? This is where the story takes a wild leap in credibility. Upon reading Lanny's column, Henry came running over waving several pieces of paper. He showed me these four pages from his family history. The first was verification of a marriage between Edward Southworth and Alice Carpenter in Leyden England on May 28, 1613. That's followed by these words:

> "These few items are all that is given in regard to the life of Edward Southworth in Leyden by the records so far published. Governor Bradford has preserved for us the only other document relating to him—a letter written by his friend, Robert Cushman, from Dartmouth England where the *Mayflower* and *Speedwell* put in there on account of the unsavory condition of the latter."

The incidence of coincidence (fate? things that make you go "hmm?") becomes even stranger. Hang in there. You may need to take notes. The letter itself is unimportant to the story, however, as Cushman merely details the difficulties and perils of traveling by sea in those days. He also chronicles his poor health, describing himself as "near dead." He accurately predicts he will never again see the New World. Both he and Southworth died shortly after.

But Alice, Southworth's wife, lived on. The history books have been kind to William Bradford, connecting him to Thanksgiving and the *Mayflower Compact*. But the historians left out a few things. Prior to either of them getting married, Alice Carpenter and William Bradford had been lovers and quite possibly had kept that romance alive even after their respective marriages. Alice's father had refused to let the governor-to-be court his daughter as he considered Southworth the more worthy suitor. Had he known about Thanksgiving, he may have chosen otherwise but lacking that foresight he chose Southworth. With Edward's passing and upon hearing of the drowning of Bradford's wife, Dorothy, the grieving widow hopped the next boat for the New World where she and Bradford were married in 1623—and she was to become known as "the mother of Plymouth colony." She was, in reality, the mother of two sons, Constant and Thomas Southworth, who, of course, came to live with her in the good governor's house.

If you've been paying attention, you will remember that Robert Cushman had left his son Thomas in the care of Governor Bradford when he returned to England late in 1621. And so it came to pass that Alice Southworth Bradford, mother of Thomas, the ancestor of Henry Southworth, became a sort of foster-mother/stepmother to Thomas Cushman, from whom I am descended.

Thus, Thomas Southworth and Thomas Cushman grew up together in Governor William Bradford's house in Plymouth, Massachusetts, in the 1620s. Nearly three hundred and fifty years later, their respective progeny, Henry Southworth and Bob Cushman found themselves working together on the same faculty at Paynesville High School in Paynesville, Minnesota. I was the first counselor hired in Paynesville. Up until then, the counseling duties were being performed by Henry.

What are the odds?

If you figure that out, go to work on this one. When I joined that faculty of about twenty-five teachers, four of us had the same birthday—October 16.

Chapter Fifteen

For as long as I can remember, I have been a people watcher. I love the limitless variety. I love the different colors, shapes, and sizes. I love the infinite diversity in other things too—flowers, birds, animals, insects—but nothing, for me, displays the heterogeneity in the world as much as the diversity of the human race. Subtle nuances make each individual so unique, so beautiful and priceless. Each has a great story to tell.

I started my people-watching career when I was about fourteen. After a shift of dispatching cabs from one to seven in the morning, I often went to the bus depot for breakfast. There were always people in the bus depot. The ones going somewhere fascinated me the most. Where were they going? Why? Were they running from someone? To someone? I knew it was none of my business. I would never have considered asking. I was too timid to strike up a conversation. But the questions—the mystery and enchantment—remained. My imagination triggered, I began to make up my own answers.

They were, of course, all borrowed from the B-movie plots I loved so much. But they satisfied my young curiosity.

60

See that young woman over there? The one with the threadbare coat and the single cardboard suitcase? See how sad she looks? How lonely? She just broke up with her boyfriend. She had moved up here from a farm near Plowville to be with him. She worked nights for Bell Telephone and lived in a basement apartment on North Main. She came home last night and found Reggie (I often used the name Reggie for roguish males, perhaps due to my familiarity with Archie comics) with another girl. She threw her friendship ring in his face, packed her suitcase and stormed out. She wandered around town all night crying. By sunup she decided she had to leave town. She had considered going back to the farm. But Mom had told her not to go to the big city in the first place. No. She couldn't face the humiliation of going back home and admitting she had failed. She would have to go somewhere it would be easier to forget Reggie. She would lose herself in an even bigger city. Minneapolis. Chicago. It didn't matter where. Just so it was far away from here. She had gone to the ticket seller, plunked her money down on the counter and said, "I want to go as far east of here as the next bus will take me."

Very rarely did Reggie show up to stop her, and, if he did, Betty (more Archie stuff) would dismiss him with a brilliant flourish of righteous indignation. Sometimes I would carry my story further and envision Betty arriving in Chicago, becoming a showgirl, getting involved with the mob, and eventually coming back home to the farm where she would fall in love with the boy from just down the road apiece. But I was usually content to just put her on the bus. That seemed to satisfy my curiosity and reverie. Once Betty boarded the bus, she was on her own.

How about that nice-looking young boy with the crewcut? He just got drafted and is headed for boot camp. He'll be in Korea pretty soon. Wonder if he'll make it? He's probably wondering that too. He looks pretty scared. I hope someone will be here to see him off. And then I'd be off on one of several scenarios I could conjure up.

And there is the couple huddled in the corner. The one with the small baby that won't stop crying. Mom is embarrassed, and Dad is angry. I think he is headed for a new job somewhere. Lots of job opportunites in the United States in the fifties, but you had to relocate. America was becoming so much more mobile. (Could anyone have guessed how much that was to change our culture in the next forty years? Well, besides Edgar Cayce?)

Occasionally my stories would take on more exotic twists like a young Dillinger on the run or a Lana Turner headed for discovery in a Hollywood soda fountain. Most of my protagonists, however, were ordinary folks living out the drama of routine lives. I guess that's what I knew best, and I didn't dare dream of anything more for myself, so I couldn't allow my heroes or heroines too much freedom to escape the mundane. It wasn't until years later I discovered how extraordinary the common is.

As a young adult, I stopped making up stories about the people I observed and I began paying closer attention to them as they appeared to actually be. I studied people. I became aware of body language, gestures, and other clues to who people are, but I was no longer interested in fine tuning my pastime to a storytelling level. Mostly I studied faces—searching for the secrets, the stories that each face held. The eyes, of course, reveal the most about a person. There you'll find the twinkle or the sadness and the occasional vacancy. More and more, I began to notice the character lines, especially those etched around the eyes and the mouth. My favorite observation posts were at the workplace and the parties I attended. I wasn't as observant at this stage as I had been earlier, and I didn't have time to make up stories. I was too busy creating my own story. For real. I had a life of my own now.

As I grew older (do men ever really mature?), my attention shifted to the folks I saw on the streets, in the cafes I frequent and, of course, the malls. Malls are the greatest people-watching venues. There are so many people. Faces still captivate me—the profusion of lines, colors, and shapes are immensely enjoyable. I am now particularly drawn to the older faces I meet. I love the deep character lines I see. These folks have so many stories to tell—stories that run the gamut of human experience and emotion. Rich stories. Dramatic stories. Tales of suspense and/or horror. Stories of romance. Great love stories. Adventures. The stories these faces mirror would dwarf all the youthful fantasies I made up back in the bus depot in Minot, North Dakota. These would be true stories, at least as true as old memories would allow them to be. These would be real stories of what really happened to all those folks who once sat in bus depots, airports, railroad stations, and on front porches all over the world.

Sometimes I find myself trying to make up a story as I did when I was a boy. I quit in futility. I know I can't begin to capture the experiences I see in these wonderful faces. I have learned that the drama of a human life is too much to be summarized in a brief story. It's too much to glean from even the most expressive faces I find. What each of us has been through, what each of us has become, cannot be captured without a full-fledged biography.

I may let my imagination ramble for a while but I give up. My heart isn't in it. Each of these people is so much more than my limited fantasies can dream up. I can't do them justice. I have discovered the remarkable does, in fact, exist in the ordinary. My heart will not allow me to discredit these amazing folks who have lived a lifetime with some feeble attempt at making up a story to go with the face. It is too disrespectful.

So now I just drink in and appreciate the beauty of these faces. I look at them. Sometimes I stare rudely. I have been struck dumb by a few. I am usually in awe of these people I've never met. Ultimately I say to myself, "What an interesting face. How much (s)he must have lived."

And I would always try to point them out to whoever I was with. That would usually be Mary, and I would always express myself with the same words, I would simply say, "Mary, look at that fascinating face over there. Isn't that great?" She always agrees and sometimes we discuss it further. Usually not. There have been occasions when I have gone from one end of the mall to the other to find Mary so I can drag her back to show her a particularly interesting face.

After these many years of observing countless faces with beautiful character lines, I have made a great and glorious discovery. One day I was looking at myself in the mirror. I was aware for the first time of the cragginess of my own visage. I ran from the bathroom and happily asked Mary, "Do you remember all those interesting faces I'm always pointing out or talking about?"

"Yes."

"I have," I shouted gleefully, "become one of them."

Corroboration came during our February golf-to-escape-the-cold-and-snow vacation to the central coast of California in 1998. For years I have been eying Greek fishermen's caps wherever I saw them but I had always talked myself out of buying one. But in a little shop by the ocean at Morro Bay, I lost the argument. The next day, wearing my new treasure for the first time, we cruised several of the smaller towns in the area. We stopped for coffee in Templeton. Shortly after we were seated a very distinguished-looking older man entered and chose the table across from us. He was the epitome of the craggy older faces I had come to love.

He introduced himself. Ron something-or-other. He claimed seventy-six years and had long, wavy gray hair. There was an impish twinkle in his eye. He wore a baseball cap, Levis, a western shirt, and hiking boots. Ron was an artist. One of his watercolors hung on the back wall of the coffee shop, a pastel of his ranch featuring a stone wall entrance. It was a beatuiful painting. Shortly after sitting down, Ron said, "You wear that hat really well. It looks very jaunty on you." He later told me I'd be an excellent subject for portraiture.

There is no longer any doubt: I am one of them.

And I'm thrilled as hell about it.

Chapter Sixteen

Somewhere in my journey, I heard a story about three children who were very good friends. They lived in the same neighborhood, played together every day, and genuinely liked each other. As they grew to junior-high-school age, some things began to change. Instead of walking a couple blocks to the neighborhood elementary school, they now waited on the corner for the bus that would take them uptown to the much larger junior high school. They were no longer in the same classroom with the same children for six hours of class each day. They no longer had recess or play time together, nor did they all have the same lunch period. Instead each followed his individual schedule as they moved from classroom to classroom each time the bell rang. Often they wouldn't even see one another from the time they got off the bus in the morning until they returned to it at three ten that afternoon.

Now they interacted with hundreds more kids. There were many more options available to them, and it seemed as if each choice made, according to their respective personalities, moved them further away from each other. As the school year progressed, they found themselves more and more distanced one from the others. They were growing up and growing apart.

Such is the stuff of life.

One day at the bus stop, an argument erupted among them. It escalated to a fist fight, which was finally broken up by the bus driver. What followed was a long period where none of them spoke to the others except to throw an insult or put the other down. Sometimes the verbal violence would be accompanied by a push or a trip and, on a couple occasions, more fists were flung. After one such fight, the boys were brought to the office of the school counselor. (I love stories where the school counselor turns out to be a hero. Perhaps that's why I remember this story even though I can't recall the source. Or maybe it's because this is the only story I know where the school counselor does something heroic.)

The counselor heard the boys out. They told of how they had once been close friends but had become bitter enemies. After hearing the entire story, the counselor thought for a while. Finally he said to the boys, "It seems to me that you can make one of three choices. You can keep fighting. You can ignore each other. Or, you can make up and become friends again." And he sent them on their way, free to select whichever choice suited them best. I've always secretly believed they chose to rekindle their friendship—but I've always been sort of a Pollyanna.

As I look at the busted, estranged, forgotten, neglected, lost, distanced and/or withered relationships in my own life, I realize those are the same three choices I have always had. They are the three choices all of us always have. In my case, there are hundreds, maybe thousands of such relationships. There are past neighbors. There are all my high school and college friends, former co-workers, and students. There are many even closer and more intimate relationships that fall somewhere on that continuum of estrangement: Dad, Mom, my brother, cousins and other relatives, and an ex-wife. In every case I have had the same three choices—to keep fighting, to ignore the other, or to make up.

I further realize I have usually made the same choice. I packed up and moved on. I have chosen to ignore and to let the relationship wither and die. By the time I had my first teaching job in Cavalier, my high school buddies were history. By graduate school, my college friends were out of my life. After being in Minnesota a few years, most everyone from North Dakota was but a memory. With each new stage of my life, I chose not to hang onto any of the old gang. I have never gone back to a homecoming at either college, and I've missed my last two high school reunions—the thirtieth and fortieth.

I tried to do the same with my family. After I moved from the house I left my nephew and three nieces, my cousins, aunts, and uncles behind. I distanced myself from my sister and my brother and finally from my parents. I put myself in a mind set where I didn't feel particularly close to anyone in my family. I chose my ex-wife's family over mine. Of course, with the divorce, I made the same choice with my ex-wife and her family.

Sometimes I hate it when I'm faced with the choices I've made and patterns I've followed in my life.

Recent events have taught me that my decisions may not have always been the best for me. I began rebuilding bridges with my parents about twenty years ago. Dad and I hadn't completed that before he died, but I think we had made enough progress that neither of us felt totally cheated. I like my mother better now and enjoy being with her more than I ever have, save for when I was really little. My brother and I have been finding more and more common ground in recent years, and the rivalry that existed between us has disappeared. I wrote about my sister earlier. That relationship has always been in a category all by itself and deserved its own chapter. I reconnected with a niece a couple years ago, and we had a wonderful few days together.

This has all been immensely satisfying, and I hunger for more. Nostalgia continues to sweep over me. A couple of years ago, I made a point to look up a couple of high school friends, a college chum, and four students from my early teaching days in Cavalier. Out of the blue, I had a phone call from Dale Brown, the former basketball coach at LSU and a lifelong friend. (We have known each other since we were five-year-old urchins roaming the streets of downtown Minot together.) This summer another former student appeared in my life again.

Each of these encounters has been thoroughly enjoyable and stimulating. They seem to have filled a void that has been empty far too long. I don't expect or desire to rekindle every past relationship, but I find myself thinking wistfully about someone from those salad days . . . I wonder whatever happened to Leon? . . . I really miss Frank. I wonder how he's doing ? Where's he at? . . . Is Chuck still alive? . . . What about Mark and Penny? . . . How could Christa have disappeared from our lives ? . . .

None of this should surprise me. The exceptions to my pattern—those I have stayed connected to like Dave, Laura, Theresa, Bill, Tom and Kelly, and Mike are among my most treasured friends. But this has been an epiphany, of sorts, and I intend to rebuild more bridges to my past, and I certainly would like to widen those where the rebuilding has already begun. This is fun. This is good for me. I will attend that fiftieth reunion in 2003.

Before I leave this topic, I can't help but expand it beyond the limits of my life. There are ramifications beyond those for individuals. Don't groups, organizations, and even nations have these same three choices—keep fighting, ignore each other, or make up and be friends? How about races and ethnic groups? Different genders? Ages? Sexual orientations? Political beliefs? Religions?

Think about it. What if Republicans and Democrats actually began cooperating and doing what is best for the people instead of making every issue a political battleground? What if Moslems and Christians began to focus on their considerable similarities rather than the minutiae that separates them? Wouldn't it be great if the Serbs and Croats would, at least, choose to ignore each other? How much more peaceful it would be if the Iraqis chose to be friends with the Kurds. Wouldn't we all be better off if gays were allowed to live their lifestyle without interference from the homophobics?

It is staggering to think how far we could take this concept.

Chapter Seventeen

I hate writing this because it shows how incredibly stupid I am. This is about the dumbest choice I ever made. It's about addictions and how I came to know so much about them. Most of what I believe I know about addictive behaviors comes from taking a close look at my own relationship with cigarettes.

I started smoking when I was in the eighth grade. I had been hanging out at the pool hall for over a year, and most of the older guys I knew smoked. As they leaned over a snooker table, cue in hand, poised for the shot, a cigarette dangling loosly from their lips, I thought it looked so cool. I remember one guy in particular. While he waited for his turn, he would sit in a chair with his head back and blow smoke rings at the ceiling. These guys reminded me of the movie stars I loved: Bogart and Cagney, George Raft, Robert Mitchum, and Robert Ryan. As I watched, I thought about John Derek playing Nick Romano, the tough Chicago kid, in *Knock on Any Door*. I wanted to be Nick Romano—to live fast, die young, and have a good-looking corpse.

One day I was shooting eight ball with an older kid in Selk's Pool Hall—"the hole." He offered me a cigarette. If anyone on the planet should never have started smoking it was me. I had been hospitalized with pneumonia several times as a young boy, and I already had bad lungs. I was subject to colds and had been diagnosed with asthma. I could have been a poster boy for the American Lung Association.

I took the cigarette without batting an eye. I put it in my mouth and picked up the package of matches lying by the side pocket. I'd been watching the guys for a long time. I knew how to do this. I cupped the match in my hands (I'm not sure why. It wasn't too windy in the pool hall.) and lit the cigarette. I was cool. I took a drag. I was suave. I inhaled deeply. I was dying. I was being burned. I wanted to choke. I wanted to cough. But that's not cool. Not in front of the guys. I was certain every one in the place was checking me out. I fought the impulse to cough. My eyes were watering as I bent over the cue ball to take a shot. I couldn't control that. After I missed I took another drag. I had to. I had to be one of the guys. More choking urges resisted. I had to fight hard to suppress that cough because it hurt so bad but those impulses had to be fought. After finishing that cigarette and watching my buddy pocket the eight ball, I went to the vending machine and purchased a "deck of Luckies" (Mickey Spillane's Mike Hammer smoked them.)

I was thirteen.

And I taught myself to smoke. I sat in my upstairs bedroom with the window upon and blew smoke out into the night. The urge to cough gradually subsided as my lungs inured themselves to the abuse I was heaping upon them. I became a smoker. I was one of the guys. I was Nick Romano walking down West Madison street in Chicago. Later on I bought a red jacket and became James Dean in *Rebel Without a Cause.*

Like all other smokers, I tried dozens of times to quit. I read the Surgeon General's report. C. Everett Koop wouldn't lie to me. He was a member of the federal government, for Pete's sake. I really did know smoking was hurting me. I knew it was killing me. But it didn't matter. Every attempt to quit or cut down found me lacking in will, judgment, sense, whatever, and I always found myself back at a pack and a half a day. Package warnings didn't stop me. Rising prices couldn't either. The best efforts of my kids sailed blithely past me like . . . well, like so much smoke. The kids were, in the late sixties, getting huge doses of anti-smoking education in grade school. Jodi would lecture me. "Dad, don't you know that smoking blackens your lungs. Let me show you these pictures. You have to quit or else . . ."

I'd heard it all. I didn't listen.

Mark's approach was much more to the point. Whenever he'd see me with a cigarette, he would just look at me and say, "You're gonna die." And he'd continue on his way to wherever it was he had been going. I ignored him, too. Thought it was cute actually.

After everyone had given up on me, I quit. On my own. One day in 1970, I just decided I was going to quit smoking cigarettes. I continued to smoke my pipes, but I never touched a cigarette for seven years. No fanfare. No big deal. And no true success. A new variation of my addiction— another form of the madness—struck in the last years of my marriage to Kris. She didn't smoke a lot, but when there was pressure and/or tension she would. The atmosphere in our house was fraught with tension, so she was smoking more than usual. I was determined not to drive the wedge be- tween us deeper, so I became certain that, when I saw her smoking, she was upset with me. (As I look back, that was probably pretty sound thinking.) This thought became an obsession with me. Her smoking became a symbol of our failing marriage. So, like a good addict, I nagged her. Easier to work her program than mine, right?

One night we were out to dinner with several friends, and Kris was smoking. I was edgy but couldn't say anything in front of our friends. Finally I thought, "Aha! I'll show her. I'll smoke, too." I bummed a cigarette from one of the ladies at the table and lit up. I probably blew smoke in Kris' face. I smoked a few more that night. Kris never said a word. I smoked more. Within a week I had reestablished my pack-

and-a-half-a-day habit. A few months later, we were divorced. She quit shortly after that, but I kept smoking until it nearly killed me.

I sure showed her.

When I started to date Mary, she made it quite clear that she wanted me to give up cigarettes. A few months into the relationship, I did just that. Mary was elated. She bragged to all her friends and relatives that I'd quit. She was so proud of me. And obviously pleased. I felt good too. Naturally, I wanted to gladden this fine lady I was dating, so, if she was satisfied, I was happy. It was hard, but I stuck to my resolve. I was not going to start smoking again. Dumb when I was thirteen. Even dumber to start again after seven years. No, sir. I wasn't going to cave this time.

The routine we had developed in our relationship had been pretty simple. She lived in a trailer in Hawick, about six miles from Paynesville. I would drive out there about seven each evening to spend time with her and her son, Troy. It was late April so we could spend a lot of time outdoors. Later we would watch television and visit. Troy's bedtime was about ten, and after he sacked out, Mary and I had some time alone. It was a nice arrangment. I was comfortable with it.

For about three days.

I couldn't handle it without a cigarette. I did what all addicts do. I started using again. But, of course, I had to sneak them. I couldn't let Mary know I was smoking. She couldn't find out. She was so proud of me. I was good at covering up. Before I left for Hawick I took a shower to remove all traces of smoke from my body and hair. I would eat something with garlic or onions and then brush my teeth and gargle with Listerine. In my car I chomped on a couple pieces of bubble gum. By the time I arrived at her door, I was pretty much sanitized and deodorized. And I'd have to lie when she asked if I had a cigarette that day. If she did suspect anything, I would deny like crazy.

I also found it hard to not smoke for four hours. I began to make up excuses—okay, they were lies—for having to leave early. My cigarettes were in the glove box, and I would light up as soon as I was out of sight from her trailer. One night, I was too tired. Another, I had paper work to do. Or I had to get up real early the next day. Each excuse was more lame than the previous one. With each one, I felt more guilty.

While driving home one night, I flashed back to my chemical dependency counselor training at The Johnson Institute in Minneapolis. I had been an observer of a therapy group for addicted teenagers. One family night, the group facilitator had everyone stand in a circle and then he asked a sixteen-year-old girl to go around the circle, look each person directly in the eye, and say, "Pot (her drug of choice) is more important to me than you are."

At the time I thought this was a great therapy technique. I didn't think anyone could do what she was being asked. Her parents and two siblings were in that group. She went around that circle with relative ease. One friend after another was informed he/she took second place to a chemical. She arrived at Mom, "Mom," she said looking at her mother eyeball to eyeball, "pot is more important to me than you are." Her older brother was next. She didn't flinch. Then her twelve-year-old sister, who was sobbing like a baby, was told she took a back seat to pot. Dad was last. Knowing the relationship I had with Jodi, I felt this would surely be a breakthrough moment. She took his hands and looked straight into his eyes. "Dad," she informed him, "pot is more important to me than you are."

She never even blinked.

I had cried the night I observed this incredulous example of addiction. And I started crying as I recalled the incident. I cried for her. But this time I was also crying for me. I wept for me because I realized I was doing the very same thing. I was telling Mary, the lady I had fallen in love with, the lady I intended to marry, "Cigarettes are more important to me than you are." It was true. I couldn't deny my behavior. Not when I was alone. I could excuse it. I could rationalize it. I could use every defense mechanism I knew, but I couldn't deny that my behavior was saying I'd rather get away so I can smoke rather than spend time with the one I love. Something had to change.

The next day I confessed my sins and let her deal with the disappointment she felt. It's what we addicts do. I couldn't give up my addiction, so I continued using and let Mary suffer the consequences. I knew she wouldn't break up with me. Loved ones almost always stick with the addict, sometimes even becoming part of the problem. I didn't quit for sixteen more years when God finally got my attention. You know the old concept about people being so dumb you have to throw a brick at them?

The brick in my case was my heart attack. The really funny thing is that when I finally quit it turned out to be relatively easy. Anytime I had the urge to smoke, I simply told myself, "that's not an option anymore." And that worked for me.

"I have seen the truth—
and it doesn't make
any sense."
—Anonymous

Chapter Eighteen

There is something wrong when . . .

During the same week, a North Carolina elementary school suspended a six-year-old boy for kissing a girl on the cheek, and the New York Supreme Court disallowed the suspension of a fifteen-year old who brought a loaded gun to his school in the Bronx.

Convicted sex-offender Christian Peter is given a chance to resurrect his football career by the New York Giants football organization, and those same Giants have banned, for life, Jeffrey Lange, a fan caught throwing snowballs toward the field during a game in 1995, from Giants Stadium.

And Latrell Sprewell, after first going to the locker room to cool off, comes back to the gym and chokes his coach and nothing is done to him. He is still playing basketball when he should be in jail for attempted murder.

And don't even get me started on Bobby Knight at Indiana.

You can readily buy assault weapons in the same states that won't allow Fourth of July sparklers on the grounds that someone could get hurt.

On his last contract as an active player, Michael Jordan made thirty-million dollars a year, enough to supply the city of Chicago with about 1,200 sorely needed teachers.

It is all right to sing a song that contains the lyric, "kill Whitey," but Michael W. Smith's "Friends" has been banned in some schools because there is a reference to God.

When Mary and I were in Rochester, New York, a few years ago, the lead story on TV warned women to be on the alert because there had been a series of assaults and rapes in one area of that city. A later feature article showed the town laying out the red carpet for former heavyweight champion Mike Tyson, who had recently been released from prison where he had been serving time for rape.

Many of the same people who oppose abortion favor the death penalty.

The justice system is no longer about justice.

Most folks are paid somewhat according to what they produce while sports stars are paid either on the basis of potential or past performance.

The average CEO makes 212 times what the average worker in the company earns.

We use a six-year-old boy who has just seen his mother drown as a political football.

Manpower, Inc., a temporary service, is the number one employer in the country.

Many whites feel we have gone too far with Affirmative Action and/or civil rights, but none of the complainers would willingly change places with a working-class black man or woman.

The United States Agency for International Development has seen the need to provide assistance within the United States, meaning there are places in this country where people are worse off than people in some third-world countries. Twenty million people in the United States live below the poverty line according government statistics.

Public outrage forced Mattell, Inc. to pull a Cabbage Patch doll from the market and offer rebates to anyone who returns one because several children had their hair pulled or suffered other minor scalp injuries. . . . The same thought process took lawn darts off the market several years ago . . .

And . . . the governement is forcing auto makers to redesign airbags because about fifty people, sixty percent of them children, have been killed over a ten-year period by these otherwise life-saving devices. . . . The city of Minneapolis has looked seriously into the problem of anchoring soccer goals on playgrounds because twenty-five children have been hurt over a twenty-year period by goals that tipped on them . . .

I support these moves wholeheartedly, but they glaringly illustrate the total insanity of the fact that we still have not been able to effectively do anything to stop the slaughter of tens of thousands of children over that same time frame, and death by gun remains the leading cause of death among teenagers.

According to an item in Chuck Sheppard's Column, "News of the Weird," Jack Tatum, the former Oakland Raiders linebacker, applied for $156,000 disability from the NFL Players Association. In 1978 Tatum made a "clothesline" hit on New England receiver Darryl Stingley's neck, causing permanent paralysis. At the time, Tatum arrogantly defended the play as legal and even warned other opponents they could expect the same kind of play. His disability application is based on the mental anguish he has suffered having to live with the Stingley incident. The $156,000 "catastrophic injury" category, the NFLPA's highest, is the same category Stingley is in.

78

Maybe this item from *Reader's Digest* summarizes what this is all about. Following a rain there was a large puddle behind a car dealership. The water was contaminated with gas, oil, and antifreeze. A salesman who was out for a brief walk (probably to get some fresh air) noticed some ducks swimming in this mess and observed, "They're killing themselves and are too stupid to know it." And then he took a last drag from his cigarette and went back to work.

Could it be that in one way or another we are all killing ourselves and are too stupid to figure it out?

Chapter Nineteen

I'm not sure where I want to go with this, but while I'm geezing (I'll explain that term in a few chapters) . . .

One Sunday evening, shortly after the horrible bombing in Oklahoma City a few years ago, I was watching *60 Minutes* and Leslie Stahl was interviewing a member of some Michigan militia group. The man was wearing army fatigues, boots, a gun belt, and he had a sash of ammunition draped over his shoulder. He looked like Rambo. Ms. Stahl asked him why his group always dressed this way and believed there was a need to do so. And the man answered, "Because we can."

"Because we can." That's the goshawfullest answer I've ever heard. And the best. "Because we can." It is both profoundly true and incredibly stupid. It's a right guaranteed us by the constitution and a shield behind which every coward who refuses to accept responsibility for his actions can hide. "Because we can" is the protector of everything that is good—and everything that is sick and perverted. Couldn't, if asked why they trot out their sleazy garbage on television, Howard Stern or Jerry Springer say "because we can"? Don't the purveyors of questionable lyrics of pop songs defend their product with "because we can"? Isn't it also true for those who crank out pornography on film, video, and the internet? Sure they can.

But why do they want to?

They can do all these things, and more, regardless of who gets hurt. Gun dealers can sell high-caliber automatic weapons to anyone with a pulse because our constitution guarantees the right to bear arms. The same freedom of speech that allows me to write this book also allows some "gansta" rapper to spew hate messages from the boom boxes of every kid who wants to listen. Freedom in America applies to us all. You can attend the church, temple, or synagogue of your choice—Roman Catholic, Lutheran, Methodist, or Krazy Karl's Kibbutz of Kooks. The laws of this country pretty much allow you to do anything you want unless there is a specific law prohibiting that act. (And that's getting pretty jerked around by the justice system.)

This is a good thing. We appreciate our freedom. We cherish it. Our freedom is the main reason most of us feel this is the greatest country in the world. It is why immigrants have been flocking to this country for over two hundred years, whether it's the European farmers of the nineteenth century or the Hmong people of the 1990s. This is the very cornerstone of America, the reason we became a nation. "Give me liberty or give me death!" shouted Patrick Henry to the Virginia Assembly. Because of the idealism of our founding fathers, we enjoy freedom of religion, freedom of speech, freedom of assembly, and a myriad of other freedoms and rights.

These were ideals in the eighteenth century and as our nation matured, the pioneers, our ancestors, worked hard to establish them as realities. It took a lot of blood, sweat, and tears to break down barriers through the years, but by the middle of the twentieth century, women were voting, slavery had legally been abolished, labor unions had narrowed the gap between haves and have-nots, people of color were playing professional sports, free public education was available to all, trusts and monopolies had been busted to level the playing field in business, and countless other rights had been gained for the average American. These were indeed Happy Days.

When I was twenty-five I was a wide-eyed idealist and romantic. John F. Kennedy had just been elected president, and the future looked mighty rosy. We were all set to break down the remaining barriers. Racism and discrimination were going to be erased. There would be no more wars. Poverty would disappear. The sexual revolution would do away with the outmoded Puritanical structure that had guilted so many. The ecumenical movement in the spiritual community would create a unity and cooperation among the churches and religious leaders. We would heed President Eisenhower's farewell warning to "beware the military-industrial complex," and we would develop a unique peace-time prosperity. We were ready, for Pete's sake, to explore outer space.

We truly were on the threshold of a new frontier. We would ask what we could do for our country. The people would speak, and our representatives in Washington, in state capitols, and county seats would listen and respond to the wishes of the people. Democracy could work. It really could! Life as far as I was concerned couldn't be better.

The sixties turned out to be the most volatile decade in our history. What started with an unprecedented and unbridled hope ended in desperate disillusionment. It was an exciting time to be alive—a time that ran the gamut of human emotion and experience.

We were so filled with optimism. And then JFK was assassinated. So was Martin Luther King, Jr. We went to war—a war that, for the first time, did not have the full support of the American people. Especially of the young men being asked to fight. There were protests and riots. Bobby Kennedy was shot. There was a war protest at Kent State University. The National Guard was called out. Several students died. So did our idealism. Gone was our hope. The dream was completely shattered.

We rebuilt as we always do. But our rebuilding was done in grief and mourning—not just for the dead, but for the dream. We rebuilt amidst confusion. Watergate. An empty end to the war. The threatened impeachment of a president and his resignation. The rebuilding during the seventies set the tone for a different kind of America. The hope and love of the sixties were replaced with fear and suspicion. We rebuilt an America of managed information and, I think, a new twist on "because we can."

It seems to me that "because we can" is no longer a ringing battle cry of freedom that sustained the hopes and dreams of the pioneers. A "because we can" born of fear has become a cloak to hide behind. I was taught that the flip side of freedom is responsibility. Now there seems to be no flip side. Too many folks refuse to accept the flip side. We have invented many new games to avoid the responsibility for what we do and, therefore, accept no culpability for the consequences of our choices. "Because we can" now implies because I can get away with it and you can't stop me. It has become the battle cry of me.

Late in 1999, *USA Today*, through their Sunday supplement, polled teenagers across the country about feeling safe in school. This was prompted by the school shootings of recent years. I copied the survey, modified it to fit my community and administered it to all the students in grades six through twelve. When asked if their behaviors are influenced by television, movies, video games, movies, and song lyrics, the local kids mirrored the national results with just over fifty per cent admitting they were, in fact, influenced by these aspects of their culture. Now certainly the media should not be scapegoated for all the violence in this country. Doesn't it make some sense, however, that if the product consumers are admitting to being influenced, the media could acknowledge their culpability and assume some responsibility for contributing to the problem. But they don't. They hide behind the first amendment and blatantly deny that their product is in any way responsible. That's a media version of "because we can."

Politicians play other versions of the "because we can" game. Politics is no longer about representing the people. It's not about doing what's best for the people. It isn't about doing the right thing. It's about which party wins. It's about staying in office. It's us against them. We shouldn't be surprised since so many of them are lawyers and learned these skills in the adversarial court system. This is just another way of refusing to take responsiblity. It doesn't matter who gets hurt by the system. This is the game they play. And they get away with it because they can. Our governor, Jesse Ventura, has a new twist. He claims the others are playing the game, and whenever anyone disagrees with him he simply says, "I'm just telling the truth." He, of course, is just pitching his views. He isn't telling some universal truth the rest of us aren't privy to. It's his way of avoiding the consequences.

And the game is played everywhere. Schools play the game. Judges do, too. Many parents play the game very well. Churches are good at it. In fact, I think we have all learned to play this game. It is so much easier to blame someone else for whatever is wrong than it is to accept responsibility for our actions. Out of our fear, our denial, our suspicions, and our delusions we continue to play the game. The real answer to Leslie Stahl's question to the Michigan militia guy (and to all the other questions and ills we see around us) isn't "because we can."

It's because we let them. We are where we are at in this society because we simply sit back and let it happen. When good people do nothing, bad things happen. We need to reclaim what is good about our society. And the way we do that is for each of us to accept full responsibility for our behaviors. We need to start telling the truth about who we are and what we do.

And to everyone who says "because we can," we need to acknowledge that it's true, they can. But we need to ask them, "Why would you want to?"

> "It's better to know
> some of the
> questions than
> all of the answers."
> —James Thurber

> "The world is too dangerous
> for anything but love
> and too small for anything
> but the truth."
> —William Sloan Coffin

Chapter Twenty

I got pretty political in that last chapter. A little danger-ous as I was always taught the two things about which you should never argue are politics and religion. Too great a risk that others will disagree. That's all well and good, but I sort of subscribe to the philosophy behind these words written by Kingsley Anis, "If you can't annoy somebody, there is lit-tle point in writing." So I'm going to ramble on a little about religion too. I have no intention of boring you with my own religious beliefs. I don't feel I have answers in that depart-ment, and if I did, they wouldn't be your answers anyway. I merely want to throw out some ideas for you to chew on. What made me think of this was a page from a daily medi-titation book, *365 Tao Daily Meditations* by Deng Ming-Dao. For you to fully understand where I'm coming from, I need to quote the entire meditation. He wrote:

> Tao is the road up your spine.
> Tao is the road of your life.
> Tao is the road of the cosmos.
> People are often confused about Tao because there are references to it on so many different levels. After all, it permeates our existence.

Indeed it might be said that Tao is existence itself. It might seem odd we can talk about Tao on a level so mundane as physical exercise and on a level as exalted as holiness itself. Those who follow Tao do not think of divinity as something "up there." They think of it as everywhere.

Tao can be tangible when it wants and intangible when it wants, too. One tangible aspect of Tao is the road in the very center of our spines. That is the path of Tao in us. It is the spirit road connecting the various power centers of our bodies.

On a philosophical level, Tao is the road through life. It is the change from one stage to another, the dealing with circumstances, the expression of our inner character against a background of nature and society. On a metaphysical level, it is the evolution and movement of the cosmos itself.

Now take these three levels—the movement of energy up the spine, the philosophical understanding of one's own path in life, and the very progression of the universe—and meld them all into one combined concept. Then you will have a glimpse of the genius of Tao.

That, my friends, is one powerful concept, and what occurred to me is that everyone might be able to think of their faith in similar terms. If you are Christian, you could interchange the word Christianity with the word Tao and have a statement fairly congruent with your thinking. Moslems can substitute Islam, Hebrews Judaism, Buddhists Buddhism, Hindus Hinduism and, quite possibly, atheists atheism. What you choose to put your faith in should be a concept that is every bit as big as Mr. Ming-Dao expresses about his. Marcus J. Berg, professor of religion and culture at Oregon State University wrote in *Meeting Jesus Again for the First TIme*, ". . . the word God refers to the sacred at the center of existence, the holy mystery that is all around us and within us. God is the nonmaterial ground and source and presence in which, to cite words attributed to Paul by the author of Acts, 'we live and breathe and have our being.'"

Think for a second about what these men are saying— the center of existence, the energy inside you, the holy mystery around us, the path of each person's life and the unfolding of the entire universe. And that's just a glimpse. No wonder J.B. Philips wrote *Your God is Too Small* when trying to make the point that the way most of us actually practice our respective faiths is way too limiting. We define our deities as beyond our understanding and then turn around and define them. We put them in a box were they are more manageable and understandable. It seems to me these men are all trying to tell us our Higher Power (and I will use that term because it is germane for so many people of all faiths) is HUGE. At the same time, there are practical applications.

When I read that my faith is about the road up my spine, I interpret it to mean that what my head thinks, my heart feels, and my body does have to be lined up. If any one of those three thing is out of alignment I feel bad. If I do something that I know is wrong—not just because I was taught wrong but because I know it in my own deepest heart it was wrong—I feel bad. I may publically defend my behavior or refuse to admit I'm wrong, but I am going to feel pretty badly about myself. Privately, I'll berate myself all over the place. When my head, my heart, and my actions are lined up, I feel in harmony with myself and, I suspect, that puts me in harmony with my Higher Power. Being in harmony with God is often described by Christians as being sin-free. At least for that moment.

Oops! It just occurred to me I'm doing what I said I wouldn't in the first paragraph of this chapter. Here I thought I was merely explaining further what is meant by the quote and, in reality, I'm expressing my personal views. No wonder people say I'm opinionated. I do this type of thing all the time. Sorry about that. I won't continue in this vein. You are intelligent enough to understand what Ming-Dao is talking about. (I really wanted to sneak in that bit about the head, heart, and body lining up. I think it's a pretty cool way of perceiving the concept about the road up your spine.) Us geezers (only a couple more chapters to a full explanation) have a way of doing that.

The other thing I did regarding what religion might do for someone, I interviewed several people (seven) and asked them each the purpose of a faith. I got some interesting observations, and I think they square pretty nicely with the quote I started with. A common answer was that faith is about having someone or something outside yourself in which to believe—a Higher Power, God, Allah, The Great Spirit. It is an acknowledgement that you don't have all the answers and that surrender to that Higher Power is essential for you to cope. Trust was mentioned by everyone. If you truly believe in your Higher Power, it means you have complete trust (faith) in Him/Her to be and do everything He/She says. That would imply we have nothing to fear in this world.

Nothing.

Let that sink in . . . When you truly believe . . .

There is *nothing* to be afraid of.

A second theme that was pretty universal is that faith is about a relationship. For that complete trust to exist, the deity has to have shown a reliability, to have demonstrated trustworthiness. That may sound off the track because we all agreed that a Higher Power does not have to prove Himself. What each person was referring to was their individual experience with diety. They were not implying a Higher Power needs to prove his/her existence. There was a knowing the Higher Power was there and could be depended upon. That knowing is probably part of that holy mystery Berg wrote about. There simply are things that can not be explained by any of us. We just know.

There was a flip side in the relationship area. As we give credibility to a Higher Power it is, in turn, affirming us as well. The atonement and forgiveness part of faith is about being lovable. We are forgiven because we are valued. And the relationship part is an all-inclusive one. Each of us is part of the family. All the major religions speak to the issue of every creature being part of the domain created by the

Higher Power. All include some form of the Golden Rule where we are encouraged to treat others the way we wish to be treated. So the relationship part of faith is about all the relationships—with the Higher Power, with self, with others.

The third common theme I heard has to do with finding your purpose in life, about following a path. This might have to do with serving others or it could be about finding your own fulfillment. It could be about both, and more. The point is there is a journey we are to travel. Some folks have a very explicit map to follow and others one much less detailed. But the map, in each case, is connected to the belief we hold about who our Higher Power is and what He/She is about.

I hope I haven't seriously offended anyone. I'm certainly not trying to persuade or dissuade anybody about their own personal belief system. I just think it's a good idea to think about what we believe. There's not enough dialogue going on about this kind of stuff. Each person I questioned about this had some variation of "nobody ever asked me that before" to preface their remarks. And each was glad they had a chance to talk about it. We need to discuss these things outside our circle of those who already think the way we do. It's much more enlightening, Don't worry so much whether or not folks agree with you. They probably won't.

And that's okay.

Chapter Twenty-One

I am curious about why God, whose other command-
ments are either about Hebrew theology, respect for one's
parents, or very specific sins would end with one concerning the neighbor's wife and servants. This was, after all,
God's Top Ten List. Of all the bad behaviors of which man is
capable and, God knows (pun intended), there are thousands. He, in His infinite wisdom, was reducing the list to
ten. These were the biggies. The best of the worst, as it were.

And right there—mixed with murder, adultery, stealing,
lying, and keeping the Sabbath holy is a mandate about your
attitude toward livestock. And it is in a prominent position.
Somewhere in my education, an English teacher told me that
when writing a series or making a list you should always
place the most important item last. The idea being that you
build from least to most important. I figured God must not
know that rule. He wouldn't consider this to be more important than having no other gods. So why? Why would God, or
any other deity, concern Himself with our thoughts about our
neighbor's stuff? What's the big deal here?

And don't even get me started on who your neighbor is
meant to be in this little treatise. I can only assume that

since we are talking about an omniscient and omnipresent diety here, one who claims we are all His children, He means everybody. He is concerned with all of mankind. I mean it might be pretty easy not to covet John Doe's wife or the stuff that belongs to "those people" on the other side of the tracks but he is talking about Bill Gates money, and he means for us not to covet Alec Baldwin's wife or Nicole Kidman's husband.

So what is all this about, this taboo on coveting? What does covet mean? It's a pleasant enough sounding word. Can it be so bad? Webster defines it as "to wish for enviously; to desire (what belongs to another) inordinately or culpably." Inordinately? Culpably? Let's see . . . inoperable, inopportune . . . ah, here it is, inordinate—"disorderly, immodestly." That sounds pretty harmless, a little risque perhaps, but not earning a spot in the top ten. I think I'll try culpably. Ah, here we are. Culpably—"meriting condemnation or blame." Now we're getting there. It's a condemnation. Surely to disobey a condemnation is a sin and that calls for blame. But something can't define itself can it?

I'm going back to covet. There were some synonyms there. Look at these: "greedy, avaricious, grasping." These are some nasty sounding words. No wonder God doesn't want us grasping our neighbor's ox or ass. I could ramble through the dictionary for hours and not come any closer than that first definition, "to wish for enviously." Envy has a deliciously clear definition, i.e., "painful or resentful awareness of an advantage enjoyed by another joined with a desire to possess the same advantage." I think that nails it. God doesn't want us playing one-up-manship with each other. Coveting isn't merely about desiring what other folks may have but wanting to beat them, to get ahead of them, to make yourself look better at the other's expense.

There is nothing wrong with wanting something. We have created an economy and culture that demands not only that we want more and more stuff but depends upon the fact we will try to satisfy those urges no matter how many plastic cards it takes. We emphasize goal setting and achievment. Success is measured for many by the accumulation of material goods. The cornerstone of capitalism is that people will pursue the highest quality goods and services and to make money (the stuff needed to buy other stuff) you have to put out a better product than your competition. All of us, to some degree, are motivated by our needs and wants.

Coveting is not about merely wanting things. The misdeed seems to be about the envy and all that goes with that. Going back to Webster, he used the term "inordinate desire" implying a yearning that is too much or misguided. Coveting doesn't seem to be much about wanting at all. Rather it is an attitude about other folks. Envy doesn't come into our hearts by itself either. Envy is almost always accompanied dutifully by resentment. Envy and resentment are two sides to the same coin. "When you hold resentment toward another," wrote Catherine Pinder, "you are bound to that person or condition by an emotional link that is stronger than steel."

I think we've finally discovered the crux of the issue. The tenth commandment deserves its place alongside murder, lying, and adultery because to covet is every bit as destructive as any of the others. In this case, however, the victim turns out to be you. Resentment, like guilt, is one of those gifts that keeps on giving. You become consumed by the feelings of resentment. The really cute twist is that, more often than not, the target of the resentment has no idea how you feel. I have known people who harbored feelings of envy and resentment toward a parent, a sibling, or some other person for a lifetime. The person who is the object of those feelings lived blissfully on, completely unaware of the resentments. The one who held the feelings seethed with the jealousy and accompanying guilt and anger. Brendan Fraser put it very succinctly when he wrote, "Whatever you hold in contempt is your jailer."

We might be better off considering the first petition of the Serenity Prayer "Grant me the serenity to accept the things I cannot change." Whatever your neighbor (brother, father, sister, cousin, co-worker, in-laws, whoever) has or does is part of that vast array of stuff in the immense category of things over which you have no control. Accepting that can help foster that attitude of gratitude that brings inner peace and contentment. Letting go of the lives of other people leaves you free to work on your own. When you do that, you can usually find satisfaction in who you are and what you have.

There's no doubt in my mind that the business of coveting belongs exactly where it is. When you harbor envy and resentment you give away all your power. You end up not happy for others' success but pretty dang miserable about your own. You don't like who you are and that seems counter productive to . . . to . . . well, to just about everything.

Chapter Twenty-Two

On October 16, 1995, I entered the most blissful stage of existence known to man. I officially became a geezer. I think I was ready for several years before that, but, according to the Geezer Information and Spiritual Resource Institute (GISRI), you are not eligible for geezerhood until you reach sixty. The GISRI is the brainchild of Dr. Gunnar Sven Lindstrom, and the "apostles" he enlisted in the late eighties. Lindstrom was chosen to be the Geezer Vizier and this devoted band of men created The Geezerei and outlined the qualifications for membership. Their work is well-documented in Lindstrom's book, *Geezerhood Examined: The Bliss Awaiting Sixty-Year Olds*. Much of what follows is my interpretation of Dr. Lindstrom's theories.

Dr. Lindstrom tells this simple story to illustrate the essence of Geezerhood:

> An old man walks into the doctor's office and the doctor asks him what the problem is. The old man says he can't pee. The doctor asks him how old he is and the old guy says 86. "Don't worry," the doctor says. "You've peed enough."

If you understand that story (and even think it's a little funny) you will understand what I have to say in this chapter. Geezers have done everything enough. That is the sum and substance—the very soul, if you will—of Geezerhood.

I qualified to be a Geezer upon reaching my sixtieth birthday. The official qualifications, as set forth by the GISRI are:

1. You must be male.
2. You must be at least sixty.
3. You must have been born in, and lived your first twelve years, in the United States.
4. You must have been married to the same woman for at least fifteen years.
5. You must have had at least one child you supported during his or her first eighteen years of life.
6. Those children must now be on their own.
7. You must have seen Snow White, any Judy Garland-Mickey Rooney, or Doris Day movie and believed at least one of the three.
8. You must have bought a house that, when you bought it, was worth more than you were.
9. You must have had an annual income that, for at least five years, was higher than your father's highest ever income.
10. You must refuse to diet, quit smoking or exercise unless you really want to diet, quit smoking or exercise.

By the way, to question any of the qualifications automatically disallows your entrance to the Geezerhood. If you truly are a Geezer you know exactly the import of each question; their ramifications and subtle nuances are instantly recognizable somewhere deep in your bones.

I passed this entrance test with flying colors on that most blissful day, October 16, 1995, and thus joined the Geezerhood, a group rife with many of my heroes. At the top of that list stood Arnold Palmer and Stan Musial. Among the many others there's Clint Eastwood, Bob Newhart, Willie Nelson, Willy Mays, Ralph Nader, Woody Allen, Harry Belafonte, and Sandy Koufax. Had they lived, surely Elvis, Buddy Holly, Carl Sagan, and Martin Luther King, Jr., would have been welcome members.

It is an august and diversified group whose contributions are legion. I am humbly proud to call myself a Geezer.

To help you better understand my status as a Geezer you may expect I will:

1. Geeze (v); speak with full authority of a Geezer.

2. Perform in a Geezeral (adj.) manner, which most definitely indicates the presence of sagacity and wisdom.

3. Act Geezingly (adv.): calmly (except on the golf course) with serenity and without concern for impressing anyone.

There are certain truths about having reached Geezerhood that automatically qualify us to Geeze, be Geezeral, and/or act Geezingly. I quote directly from Dr. Lindstrom's book because I cannot possibly put these principles as succinctly and eloquently as he. Before becoming a Geezer, it would have been important for me to try being more clever than the good doctor but that is no longer the case. It doesn't matter who gets credit. Some of the more important truths are:

"Geezers have sinned so frequently and have received so little in return they've quit sinning from sheer exhaustion."

"The Bliss of Geezerhood is not possible if not preceded by the pains of experience."

"The following phrase epitomizes Geezerhood: Enough Pain and Bullshit Already!"

"Geezerhood is an internalized ethic based on a saturation of mistakes and sins resulting first in fatigue and then in enlightenment."

"Any system that works is almost a miracle."

"Smart doesn't count for much."

"Experts aren't."

"We don't condemn any behavior; we just look back and remember the godawful messes we got into when we tried that same behavior."

"This is it, LIFE! We understand. You've given us your toughest shots. We bit, we took on the whole catastrophe and we survived. The surprise is gone. Only the bliss remains.

There are a few tenets upon which I feel the need to elaborate a bit. Dr. Lindstrom states "Women are mysteries to

Geezers and will remain mysteries. We have no idea what women are thinking or why."

I think this is a very important distinction to make, and it is the primary reason why there has never, in the entire history of human beings, been a single case of a female Geezer. I have been married to two women, the first one for nearly twenty years and to my current wife for twenty plus. My two daughters are grown women. My granddaughter is developing into a young woman. I have had many female friends my entire life. The majority of my clients when I counseled were female. My formal education was mostly about psychology, sociology, and other behavioral sciences. And I've read *The Feminine Mystique*. This most assuredly qualifes me, as much as any man, to understand women.

And I have no clue.

When I tried sharing some of the concepts from Dr. Lindstrom's book with any of my women friends, I got that same look a man gets when he tries explaining to his wife or girlfriend why the Three Stooges are funny. Women don't get the Stooges and they don't get geezerhood either. Geezerhood is primarily a state of mind and the state of the female mind is just incomprehensible to us. We tried. Oh how we tried. For forty-five years we tried.. And then Geezerhood arrived and, like with everything else, we said "Enough Already."

Another primary truth identified by The Geezerei that needs further attention is:

> "We realize we never had any power and/or control; our lives have worked out to this point and we haven't the vaguest idea what the hell happened."

We have spent our entire lives planning things. We've planned family vacations. We've planned father-son outings. We mapped out many a business meeting. We had carefully laid out plans for how our lives would work out. We planned budgets, picnics, parties, and surprises. And it became an obsession. Everything had to be planned. And the plan had to be followed. If something went wrong there was plan B as a backup. And finally, with Geezerhood comes the realization that every plan we ever put on paper (or in our computer) was so far off from what actually happened that it became clear we never had any control in the first place. Murphy has pretty much had it right all along.

The third Geezerei truth I'd like to expand upon is this: "We are not certain of anything."

Most of what I believed at any given point in my life has been proved wrong. Or at least partially wrong. The point is that I, like every other young adult, thought I was pretty smart. And I started out to really make some changes in the world. I had some answers and wanted to pass my ideas on to my students. I served as a deacon in the church and taught Sunday school. I even preached a few sermons when the minister was absent. I took an active interest in politics. I was very opinionated, and I backed up my opinions with mountains of data. I was very sure of myself on nearly every subject.

As time elapsed I became less and less certain. New information and experience showed me there were many shades of gray I had overlooked. I still held my opinions but viewed them as just that, opinions. More and more, it seemed that absolutes only existed in the mind of God and I had no access to that. I still suspected that maybe I had a clue. But certainty? No way. Not about anything. I know what seems to be true for me at any given point but that's about it.

So what it all comes down to for me is this:

I'VE HAD ENOUGH!

I've had enough competition. I've had enough attention. I've had enough people telling me what to do. I've had enough complications, expectations, guilt, and judgments. I don't need any more parties or presents. I have enough stuff. I've had enough opportunities. (And I've blown enough of them, too.) I've had enough meetings. I've belonged to enough organizations. I've had enough religion. I've made enough plans. I've had enough formal education. I've simply had enough of all those things that I believed, in my younger years, you were supposed to do and have.

I'm tired.

But what I haven't had enough of are things like bliss, serenity, love, freedom, friendship, and spirituality. That's what I need for the rest of my life. That and permission to continue geezing.

Joseph Campbell encouraged us to "follow our bliss." Webster defines that as spiritual joy; rapture. I think of the precious few moments in my life when I think I have experienced rapture, and I want more of those moments. I have always considered *The Serenity Prayer* to be one of the most beautiful and powerful pieces ever written. I want that serenity to accept the things I cannot change, that peace that passeth all understanding. (Even if I have to give up golf to fully achieve it.) I need that peace. Desperately. There is so very much I can't change and don't understand. And I want to be comfortable with that. You can never be loved enough or have too many friends. I believe I have been richly blessed in this area, but I still want all I can get. And I want to feel free. As free as the birds and all other creatures. I want to be free to continue developing my relationship with God, as I understand Her/Him. It has been over twenty years since I first really felt the intense closeness of that relationship and much of those twenty years has been spent developing that relationship. I want to continue that.

That's what this last phase of life is about for me—just geezing. My life has been richly blessed beyond any expectation or my wildest imagination. I invite you to stick around for the rest of my journey. It's going to be fun.

Chapter Twenty-Three

Flying from Los Angeles to Denver in 1995, I found myself seated next to an attractive young woman. I noticed she had three books with her. We exchanged a few pleasantries but traveled mostly in silence until the snack break. She was reading Ann Rice's latest vampire novel, and I was wrapped up in Robert Fulghum's *From Beginning to End*. Over peanuts and soda, however, we struck up a conversation.

"You read a lot?" I asked.

"I go in streaks," she answered. "I'll read everything in sight for a couple months and then nothing at all for the next several months. Then I repeat that pattern."

"I'm sort of like that, too," I offered, adding, "and when I'm on a reading streak, I'll usually have three or four books going at a time."

She acknowledged that she did that too. Having found some common ground, we continued chatting amiably about books and other stuff while we munched away at the feast prepared for us by United Airlines. Among other things I learned that Heather (my seat mate) worked for someone who had written some books, and she learned I had recently published my first book. I just happened to have a copy in my carry-on luggage. (Imagine that!) I dug one out and handed it to her. Some impulse made me say, "Here. You can have this."

"No. That's all right, but I would like to read a few chapters."

"Fine." I suggested the chapter about my childhood and current Charlie McCarthy dolls. While she read, I busied myself with a crossword puzzle.

She liked the story, but confessed, "I don't know who Charlie McCarthy is." I explained he had been a dummy for Candace Bergen's dad, who was a famous ventriloquist. We talked more. Again she mentioned working for someone who had done some writing. I suggested another story to her. She read. We talked. This pattern was to continue until we reached Denver. In the conversation, I mentioned I had published my book myself, not having been able to interest a publishing company. She countered that by telling me her boss had written five or six books before she got published. In nearly every snippet of our conversation, she said something about her boss and her writing. She must have wanted to tell me about her boss.

She was saying all the right things. She really liked what she was reading. She asked if my "wonderful insights" came to me during an event or not until years later. How discerning and perceptive I thought she was to recognize my brilliance. Let's face it. I was an old geezer being flattered by a pretty young girl. Few of us old guys can resist that. She completely won me over when she said, "If the offer is still open, I would like to keep this book. I really want to read the rest of it."

Naturally, I agreed, and, as we began our descent to Denver's new airport, I finally had the presence of mind to ask, "What sort of stuff does your boss write?"

"Well . . . uhm . . . aah . . . Danielle Steele," Heather answered.

"Oh," I reacted, "she writes romance novels."

"She is Danielle Steele. I'm a personal assistant for Danielle Steele."

Heather and I parted company in Denver. She connected with a flight to Dallas while I proceeded to Minneapolis. I didn't expect to hear from her again, and I never did. But I can't help but wonder how we happened to be placed together for that two-hour interlude—she working for the most widely-read author in the world and me looking for every opportunity to further promote my book with the hope that some miracle will happen.

> "The great big secret
> to life is that
> there is no secret.
> The gift is there.
> You need only see it
> to have it."
> —Rusty Berkus
> *Life is a Gift*

Chapter Twenty-Four

I sent that first book to dozens of people who I thought might help promote it. It went to newspaper, radio, and television personalities in the Twin Cities. I sent it to institutions, libraries, and schools where it seemed appropriate. I got help from my friends, family and my editors. *It's So Simple . . . It Just Ain't Easy* was being distributed all over the country to folks who, it seemed to me, might just take a liking to it and want to help further promote it.

And I thought big. I sent it to Oprah. Twice. I mailed copies to each of my favorite authors: Robert Fulghum, Richard Bach, and Anne Wilson-Schaef. None of these promotional seed books fell on fertile soil. I wasn't getting any help.

It all seemed so futile. Not one single sale resulted from all this effort. I even got an excellent review in *The Phoenix,* a Minneapolis-based newspaper circulated in recovery and spiritual circles. Great review. No sales. Just as the publisher's rejection letters had been disheartening earlier, this lack of response was putting me in a funk. Maybe my writing isn't that good. I'd sent out over one hundred books and my assumption was that none of them had been read. I had received a couple of polite letters: "Mr. Fulghum is on a sabbatical. He's out of the country for the next eight months but I will see to it he gets your book as soon as he gets back."

About the time I had become certain the only ones who would ever read my book were family and close friends, I got a gift via my answering machine. I had been golfing and came home to find the machine winking at me. Not unusual. I pushed the listen button and rather absently listened as the machine kicked in. "Hello, Bob Cushman. This is Richard Bach. I got your book . . . " I stared in disbelief as the machine droned on. My heart was in my throat. My stomach was acting like the gymnasts you see doing their floor exercise.

What? Who? What's this? Is this a joke? Or am I hearing right? Richard Bach! Richard Bach is talking to me on my answering machine. He's talking about my book. I couldn't slow my mind. It was racing like crazy. I was listening—but not listening because so many thoughts were flying through my brain. My left brain was competing with my right brain. My head was fighting my heart. The Irish in me was quarreling with the English. This just couldn't be. But it was. NO! Yes, it is. It's him.

The machine stopped. I sat in my kitchen. Stunned. Utterly stunned. "Richard Bach had called me. Richard Bach, the author I most admire and whose work I absolutely adore. In my opinion, the best author in the whole world. Richard Bach, the author of *Forever* and *There's No Such Place as Far Away*. And he called me. He actually called *me*. What had he said? I think he liked my book. I better listen again.

Hello, Bob Cushman. This is Richard Bach. I got your book—a lovely title and a beautiful comment about writing and your writing in particular. You're very smooth and very easy with words. Just for fun, I have a name to suggest to you and that is Will Schwalbe. He is editorial director at William Morrow and Company, 1350 Avenue of the Americas, New York, New York 10019. Maybe it would be interesting to send a copy—if you want to—to Will with a letter saying that I read your book, and I thought it was great fun and I thought that, before you send it to someone else. You should send it to him. He's a dear soul, and he's also very straight, and he'll tell you whether he thinks it will work for him or Morrow. I know you didn't ask for suggestions but I was just so touched with the book that it would sure be nice if other people could read it. So, whether or not you do, I really enjoyed the book and thank you so much.

"My God! Richard Bach liked my book. He was touched by it. He thought it great fun. And he actually called me. ME! The best writer in the world liked my book, and he took the time to call me to tell me. WOW! I had to hear it again. I listened several times. Sure enough. Each time he enjoyed, was touched by, and thought my book was great fun. I transcribed the message into my computer where I could make dozens of copies if I wanted. I recorded it on a different tape—one I could save forever and listen to again and again.

I called Mary and told her about. I called several friends and family members. And I played the tape for everyone who entered our house. I wanted everyone to hear these beautiful words from Richard Bach. "Hey, you, stranger on the corner. C'mon over and listen to this tape. Richard Bach enjoyed my book. Whaddya think of that?"

Richard Bach liked my book. It no longer mattered that no one had chosen to publish it. It no longer mattered that none of the promotional books I'd planted yielded any fruit. Richard Bach liked my book, and that was good enough for me. It *was* a good book. It *was* well written. Richard Bach had said I had an easy way with words and that my book was fun and enjoyable. And Richard Bach is the best writer on this planet. He wrote *Jonathan Livingston Seagull* and *Illusions* for crying out loud.

I was ecstatic. I still am.

Will Schwalbe? I never heard from him.

And I don't really care.

"I have always been
delighted at the
prospect of a new day,
a fresh try,
one more start,
with perhaps a bit of
magic waiting
somewhere behind
the morning."
—J.B. Priestly

Chapter Twenty-Five

Today a waitress gave me my bill and jokingly said, "Sorry, but I have to do this."

I smiled and replied, "That's okay. Everybody has to make a living."

As I sipped my coffee, the enormity of that exchange began to spill over me. Probably some coffee, too, but that's another story. And for that I'd defer to my wife who would be more than happy to tell you what a slob I am. She can write her own book. Back to my story. As I sat there I wondered. How many people were involved in her serving me a cinnamon-streusel muffin and a cup of coffee?

I began with the obvious. I have been retired from counseling for nearly three years. Teacher retirement funds are scant. I can't live the way I want on my meager monthly pittance. To indulge myself in an occasional muffin and cup of coffee, I needed to "make a living." I had recently taken a job at a local motel so I could afford the extras I wanted in my life.

Patrice, the waitress, was about eight-months pregnant at the time. She certainly needed to make a living and needed all the extra money she could get to meet the needs of the baby due to change her life forever. So much for the obvious. Now let's start to stretch our thinking a little. Okay, a lot.

The people who own the restaurant, the cooks, other waitresses, and bus boys are all, in some teeny measure, "paid" by this little transaction. Perhaps the building is leased and there is a landlord involved. Almost certainly there is a bank with all its employees and investors in the picture somehow. Granted, we are talking about the minutest inclusions here. But we are also talking big picture. In the giant scheme of things, what each of us does ultimately influences everyone else. Our global economy is entirely based on all these gazillion little transactions that take place every day, all the time in every nook and cranny in the world. So, I'll continue.

There are the salespeople who sell to the restaurant that particular brand of muffin. They are created by bakers somewhere in ovens that are manufactured who knows where. These ovens are sold by representatives of the manufacturer. These companies collectively have thousands of employees. All, to some degree or other, are dependent upon this simple and pleasant exchange between Patrice and me.

And, of course, there are the farmers who grew the grain and sugar, milked the cows to provide the milk and cheese, tended to the chickens who laid the eggs, and otherwise produced every ingredient that made up that tasty muffin I so thoroughly enjoyed this morning. By the time we include the coffee, we must surely, if we hadn't been before, be now speaking of an international incident.

And all these people—waitresses, farmers, manufacturers, herbalists, and whatever else—have families to which they belong. By the time we tote it all up, we are talking of thousands (millions?) of folks from several countries and perhaps a dozen or so ethnic groups and cultures. We have crossed a wide spectrum of creeds and religions. Most certainly every color has been part of all this. What a wonderfully diverse group has been involved in this teeny little piece of business. And, of course, the billions of similar ones that occur so routinely in our world.

We are so interconnected in this space we occupy called earth. We are inexorably linked, one to the other. We get textiles from Bangladesh, as well as, wool from Bolivia and cotton from Israel. Some of our rubber comes from Sri Lanka. That cup of coffee I had may have come from Brazil or Kenya. The bananas Mary slices on her cereal every day could come from Belize, and the sugar I put on mine from the Dominican Republic. And the television that brings us our morning news and weather is likely from Taiwan. I am in absolute awe of the delicate intricacies by which our lives are intertwined.

Given this total interdependence and connectedness that exists as the natural order of things on this planet—this oneness that crosses all differences—this unity that is the very fabric of our existence—I can't believe that, after all the lessons our human experience has shown us, so many still choose to focus on the petty differences. That we would choose prejudice, discrimination, violence, and hatred instead of this natural harmony is so sad.

We all need to share a cup of coffee.

Chapter Twenty-Six

Falling in love can be the most wonderful experience in the world. It can also be one of the most painful. I remember the first serious crush I ever had. I was in the fourth grade. Her name was Darlene. I had just moved into the neighborhood and started a new school. And there was Darlene. She was adorable. And I was in love. I handled this in the suave and sophisticated manner that nine-year-old boys usually do. I teased her. I watched her from afar. And never, ever, let on that I liked her.

What followed was a series of girls for whom I felt a combination of affection, lust, and fear. There was Janice, Gail, Delores, Doris, Kay, Cleo, Janet, Judy, Shelley, Shirley, and a few others I've long since forgotten. Ah, yes. I fell in love on a regular basis throughout junior high and high school. But I never did anything about it. Too scared. I loved them all, to be sure, but I was afraid to ask any of them to go out with me. I had zero confidence in and no respect for myself. I knew there was no way any of these wonderful girls would consider going out with me. The fear of rejection took its ugly place in my life. To some degree or other, that bogeyman has remained steadfastly by my side for over forty years now.

The desire to date was strong. Many of my friends were dating. Going steady even. And, as was common, they would tell anyone who would listen of their romantic adventures. I know now that they lied through their teeth, but I eagerly ate up these tales. And I wanted stories of my own to tell. And lots of these girls I secretly loved were good friends. In fact I became their confidant. Several sought my advice on how to deal with their boyfriends. Janice would talk to me about Ken; Janet and I discussed Boyd. I really hated that but never let on. That was at least a link to these girls. It was better than no relationship at all.

The first time I actually got serious enough and brave enough to act on it, I asked Jackie Cochran to go to the prom with me. We were both juniors. Neither had any dating experience. We began a steady relationship that lasted over two years. I think we were both afraid no one else would be interested. That was sure true for me. I truly believed that I was in love with Jackie. After our freshman year in college, she moved fifty miles away. She met another guy. She broke my heart.

But I was hooked on love. I fell in and out of love scores of times over the next couple years. Some I dated. Others I didn't. Some were dating friends. Others I was scared to ask out. I was so fearful of rejection. But I loved them all. There was Kathy, Mary Lynn, Vonnie, Pat, Mary Lou, Claudette, Mickey, Gail, and Margo among others. Finally I met Kris who was to be the love of my life for over twenty years.

By the time that relationship ended, I truly had experienced love from every angle. Like Joni Mitchell, I had "looked at love from both sides now." I knew its bliss, its intimacy. I knew its pain and disappointment. I had experienced rapture and utter despair. Love had taught me about unconditional acceptance and about total rejection. The highest moments of my life and the lowest had been those I shared with those I had loved. Try hundreds of sides, Joni!

"Love isn't easy." Carl Sandburg wrote, "It costs."

There's another old song that extols the virtue of love "the second time around." I found a new love—my current wife, Mary. I was every bit as much in love with her as I had been with my first love or my last. It was just as romantic, just as exciting as any previous love had been. Plus I had all this experience to put into this new relationship. I was determined to use all this experience to make certain that things would work out better than either of our respective first marriages had. This love was to be more mature. We became better friends than I had with any previous love. This relationship began to take on comfortable and familial qualities. I was determined not to make the same mistakes I had in my first marriage.

And I don't think I did. I made brand new mistakes this time.

Through the years we did become comfortable together. Things began to take on a familiarity. Perhaps too much so. We survived many crises together early on, and our love and respect for each other grew with each one. Our friendship remained fast, and our love for one another grew deep. In spite of that, a distance began to develop between us. A certain amount of complacency set in. Like so many couples growing older together, we began to take each other for granted. Things became more routine and predictable. We stopped working on our relationship. And a relationship not actively pursued will always atrophy to some extent.

But the most amazing thing happened. Just as my mid-life crisis was about to overlap early senility, I fell in love again.

With Mary.

It didn't just happen overnight, but it happened quite fast. At our age you don't always have a lot of time, you know. It was precipitated by a crisis, the details of which aren't very important. But both Mary and I recognized that we really did, in fact, love each other very much and that our love had been neglected. We further recognized that we wanted to recommit ourselves to each other. I expected things to develop in a slow and steady pattern. That hasn't been the case.

I fell in love again.

111

With my wife.

There's a chapter later in this book where I'll discuss the many words that fascinate me—words that are extremely rich in meaning. So rich, in fact, that it takes a paragraph to explain their meaning. One such word is pentimento. I discovered this word while reading the epilogue to Robert Fulgham's *True Love*. He found it in Lillian Hellman's biographical reflection *Pentimento*. Miss Hellman wrote, "Old paint on canvas, as it ages, sometimes becomes transparent. When that happens it is possible, in some pictures, to see the original lines: a tree will show through a woman's dress, a child makes way for a dog, a large boat is no longer on an open sea. That is called pentimento because the painter 'repented,' changed his mind. Perhaps it would be as well to say that the old conception, replaced by a latter choice, is a way of seeing and then seeing again. . . . The paint has aged now, and I wanted to see what was there for me once, what is there for me now."

And I know that's what happened to me. The love had been there all along, painted over by many scenes. But it was there. Thank God for pentimento. I was able to see something—and then see it again, for the first time. Recapturing the magic of our love seems to have happened quite easily. Maybe it's maturity. Maybe it is because we don't have a lot of anticipated outcomes and are more willing to just experience each other every day. Whatever it is, I am so thankful. I am sixty-four years old and I'm in love again.

I started this chapter saying that falling in love can be the most wonderful experience in the world. For me, that's more true now than it was at any of the earlier times in my life. I think I'll finally get this right.

I certainly hope so.

Chapter Twenty-Seven

I sat in my classroom on the second floor of Cavalier High School. It was September of 1958, and I was about to start my first class—third period senior English. I had survived supervising first period study hall. It was now the middle of period two, my prep period, and I sat there thinking about what lay ahead. This was to be my room for the next school year. My kingdom where I would hold forth over two periods of tenth-grade English, two of twelfth-grade English, and an elective speech class. All here in this room with dirty yellow walls and faded brown desks. I was excited. I was scared to death.

Only a month earlier, I had been hired for this job, and I was no more prepared to teach English than I would have been for a moon launch. I hadn't even had an English class since high school. My college major was social studies, but I had a speech minor, and in those days, that qualified me to teach English in North Dakota. Right! I didn't even feel qualified to teach speech. Or social studies, for that matter. Hell. I didn't even really want to teach. I wanted to go back into radio announcing. That's where my heart was at, but I hadn't got any good offers for that. And I was, after all, now a responsible adult with a wife and a child. Radio was insecure. Maybe even frivolous. Teaching was solid. Conscientious. Mature. Dedicated.

I sat waiting to embark on a career I was only mildly interested in pursuing and ill-prepared to do. But I was undaunted. How hard could it be to teach high school kids? I was smarter than them. I could just stay a few pages ahead of them in the text, and I'd be just fine. Besides, I had all those teacher preparation courses on "how to teach"—methods courses. Isn't it amazing how naive one can be at twenty-two.

In the teacher workshop at the end of the previous week, a few of the veteran teachers had clued me in on some of the things I could expect. They warned me of the sophomore class, which had earned a rowdy reputation through the years. They identified individuals I should be wary of. Over forty years later, I can still remember those names. That's not a statement of pride. It's an admission of shame—shame that I allowed those veterans to prejudice me to that point that those few students remain vivid in my memory bank while most of their classmates names and faces have slipped into unreachable recesses of my mind.

I really wish people wouldn't pass along their judgments. Teachers are known for it. Every group of young people I ever faced had been preceded by the evaluations of those teachers who had them earlier. And it never proved helpful. It only planted seeds of negativity and bias. It did nothing to guide me, and it certainly was no favor to the kids.

So, as I waited for my first class, my head was swimming with doubts about my career choice, mixed feelings about my ability to be successful, and prejudices of the kids I was about to meet. Great! The big question was *can I handle the kids*? All of the methods classes I had taken and all of the experienced teachers I had met had advised getting absolute control right away. "Be tough at first." "Show them who's boss right away," is what I learned. "You can ease up later if you like." I was convinced that was the way to go. Start firm. Take control. Be tough.

That's where my thoughts were when interrupted by the bell ending second period. Moments later, a boy sauntered into the room. A big boy. A really big boy. No. This was a young man. I'd guess about six feet two inches and 220 solid pounds. He had a five o'clock shadow at 10:00 A.M.. His hair was unruly. He had broad shoulders and a barrel chest that narrowed to a thin waist. His short-sleeved tee shirt revealed massive biceps and forearms.He looked to be fully capable of fighting a bear with a switch.

And winning!

As others began to drift into the room, he slouched into the first chair in the row directly in front of my desk. He grinned and said, "Hi."

I'm no genius, but I instantly knew that all I had learned in the methods classes and all the advice from the seasoned teachers was not going to work for me. How was I going to show them who was to be boss? How was I going to be tough? Hell. Forget the other thirty kids filing into the room. When push came to shove I wouldn't even be able to handle him. No. Tough wasn't going to work for me.

Not then. Not ever. That flash of insight triggered the most important teaching decision I ever made. This young man wasn't even one I'd been warned about. And he definitely wasn't the biggest student I was to face in my thirty-four-year career. This perception came to serve me well. Teaching is not about fear and intimidation.

After I introduced myself to that first class, I told them, "there will be one rule for this classroom. We will all respect each other." For the next three and one-half decades I told every class I faced essentially the same thing.

Fear and intimidation don't work. Threats and coercion don't work. They don't work in the classroom. They're not effective in the workplace or in government. These tactics don't work in any relationship. It's not good parenting, and it doesn't make for happy marriages. When I was growing up, I feared my teachers and others I was taught to respect. This included policemen, judges, ministers, and a good deal of the rest of my elders. However, I'm quite sure I did not respect them. I was just afraid of them. And I most definitely felt threatened by them. These were folks I believed could hurt me. They often doled out punishment. I did not want to be punished, so I was scared of them for what they had the power to do to me.

I think respect is an entirely different concept.

I did not want students to be afraid of me. I never wanted to demand respect. I wanted to be respected for who I was, not feared for what power I wielded. Respect, for me, has to be a mutual thing. It has to go both ways or it doesn't truthfully exist. I tried—and, God knows, I often failed—to treat each student with the dignity that every human being deserves. I tried not to judge them. I eschewed labels. Labels are the great promoters of discrimination in the world and cannot exist where respect is present. In short, I tried to be their friend. I didn't want to be a buddy, a pal. I wanted to be a true friend—someone who genuinely cared about them. I tried to let them know that I believed that each of them was important. Who they were, what they believed, what they had to say was valuable. I was willing to listen to them.

I think it worked pretty well for me.

Chapter Twenty-Eight

In *It's So Simple . . . It Just Ain't Easy,* I wrote that one of
the stories I really wanted to tell was that of Jim Puppe, a
former student in Cavalier. I have told Jim's story, up to a
point, to scores of classes and other audiences. The reason
I never finished was because I didn't know what had happened to Jim. But even without an ending, his story is a
wonderfully inspiring one. The fact that the audience was
left hanging may have added to the inspirational value of the
story. I admit I embellished the story for dramatic effect.
And since I have told the embellished version so many
times, I no longer can distinguish the fact from fiction. All
legends grow in stature with the passing of time and heroes
become more heroic with each telling of their tale. Henry
Milkey, who was the hometown hoops hero when I grew up
and, arguably, the best basketball player in North Dakota
history, recently told my brother, "I'm glad they don't have
televised records of all my games because I just keep getting
better and better." I've always looked at that as a storyteller's license. I also want to make it clear that I always
remained true to the spirit of the story.

Here then, dimmed by the years and fuzzied by my need to dramatize—is Jim Puppe's story as I have always told it. Jim was a pretty typical student in my history classes, and I think his performance was less than remarkable in most other classes, too. And I even remember seeing on his permanent record an IQ score that fell in the average range. In athletics and other co-curricular activities, he always gave one hundred percent, and he had many good moments, but he wasn't what anyone would call the "star" of the team. His overall performance was, like most of the rest of us, pretty ordinary.

But none of us is merely ordinary or only average. We all stand out in some area of life. Each of has our own unique gifts. We are all rather smart. We are all rather dumb. It depends a good deal on what issue is at hand. Anyway, Jim Puppe did something pretty remarkable when he was a sophomore in high school. At least his biology teacher told me it was remarkable. By today's standards and in light of the technological advances of the past forty years, it probably doesn't seem so special. In 1960, this was huge. What Jim did was keep some frogs alive all winter.

Jim had chosen that for a biology project. His teacher told him it couldn't be done because, when held captive, frogs refuse to eat. I don't even know if that's true or not. Never have. I guess I thought it unimportant. Whatever. Jim went ahead and kept those frogs alive all winter anyway. Having grown up on a farm, he had seen medicine blown through a tube into the stomachs of cattle. He simply applied that principle to his frogs. Tiny bits of food. Tiny tubes. And it worked. That's genius. He saw a relationship between something impossible and something quite common. He added a little creativity and did the impossible.

Two years later, Jim was considering his future. He wanted to be a doctor. He wasn't getting total support for that idea. Some folks, who were only looking at his average high school record, were discouraging him from pursuing something so challenging as medicine. Jim applied to the University of North Dakota's pre-med program anyway. I

118

like that. I've always believed people should set their sights as high as they dream. At least then you always know you gave it your best shot. That seems to be a much healthier approach than that taken by those who, at fifty or sixty, lament, "I could have been . . ."

He was turned down by the university. Undaunted, he applied at and was accepted by a small two-year college, Bottineau School of Forestry, where he completed his general education requirements. He worked very hard and did well enough to now get accepted into pre-med at the university. While he was pursuing pre-med, I enrolled in grad school, also at UND. Our paths often crossed, and we had many opportunities to chat. His dream was alive and well. He was working his butt off—both in class and at the job he held at the university hospital. His day consisted of classes, work, and studying. It was paying off. He had applications being considered at several schools of medicine, and he was anxiously awaiting answers. I lost track of Jim again for over thirty years so I never knew how he made out. What I did know is that when I got sick I wanted someone with Jim's attitude and integrity to care for me. Fortunately that was what I got, both with my cancer and my heart attack—people like Jim.

I continued to tell Jim's story, even without the ending, to every class I taught and as part of many presentations I gave. Okay, it's not Helen Keller or Mother Teresa, but it is in the class of some of the sports heroes like Calvin Murphy and Mugsy Bogues, who, despite their lack of height, had successful NBA careers, or Jim Abbott and Mel Gray, who both played major league baseball with one arm. Murphy's story sums up the attitude I'm talking about nicely. One time, his college coach was asked, "Do you really think Calvin can make it in pro-basketball? He's only five-foot eight."

The coach answered, "I know, but he thinks he's six-five." That's who Jim Puppe is. He may have looked ordinary to a lot of others, but he saw himself as having what it took. He knew he was capable of fulfilling his dreams and reaching his goals. The obstacles in his way were immaterial and ignorable. It's like the bumblebee. All the scientists who study this little creature agree that his small wings are unable to lift his body weight, making it impossible to fly. The bee is oblivious to this scientific data, so he just goes ahead and flies anyway.

A couple months after *It's So Simple . . . It Just Ain't Easy* was published, I got a phone call from an old friend in Paynesville, Fran Hedlund. "I know where Jim Puppe is." she told me. I couldn't believe it. (I have to confess to some stupidity. Fran's daughter, Jean, had told me this when she was in my class at school, but I didn't follow up at that time. So this was actually the second time I couldn't believe it.) All these years I thought I had no ending for this story and it was only a few blocks down the street. It turns out that Fran's son, Rick, married a cousin of Jim's. Talk about your six degrees of separation.

So I got a phone number from Fran, and called Jim and arranged to meet him in Fargo, North Dakota, where he now lives. We had a great reunion, and he finished the story for me. I know you'd like to hear that he's chief of staff at John's Hopkins, or Chicago Hope, or something like that. Sorry. Jim didn't get accepted into any of those medical schools. After graduating from college, he joined the army and served in Vietnam. And then he moved back to North Dakota, where he took a job with the Veterans Administration in Fargo.

Are you disappointed? I hope not. Jim is still a hero and an inspiration to me. He will never have to look back and wonder. He just ran into a rubber tree plant that was too big to move so he went on with his life. (If that reference is too obscure, listen to some Sinatra.)

"An oak tree and a reed
were arguing about
their respective
strength. A strong wind
came up and
the reed survived by
bending with the wind.
The mighty oak stood
firm and was torn up
by the roots."
—Aesop

Chapter Twenty-Nine

In May of 1967, Henry Southworth, Curt Strand, and I, as senior-class advisors, were chaperoning the senior class trip to Taylor Falls. As we boarded the bus, Mr. Southworth advised the students this was a school function and, as such, would be governed by school rules and regulations. Among the specifics he covered was the rule against smoking. And to this he added, "I know some of you will try to sneak a smoke, so be sure none of us sees you. Get out of the park." I had an eerie feeling that was a mistake.

After the picnic lunch was over and students scattered over the grounds, Curt and I decided to go to a cafe across the street for a cup of coffee. As we enjoyed our coffee, we discussed how Henry's little addendum to the smoking rule actually gave kids permission to smoke. We were more than a little uncomfortable with it, since we were not only both smokers ourselves at the time, but we were having a cigarette with our coffee. We certainly were hoping we wouldn't see any of our kids smoking. You know by now where this is going, don't you?

Through the window I saw Tom, Dick, and Harry (not real names) coming through the park gate headed for the cafe. Each had a cigarette dangling from the corner of his mouth. They came in the door. Only Harry bothered to remove his cigarette as they passed our booth. "Now," we asked each other, "what do we do?" To further complicate the dilemma, Harry was a baseball player while neither Tom nor Dick had participated in an extra-curricular activites throughout high school. To turn them in would surely result in Harry being declared ineligible the rest of the season, but no punishment at all would be administered to the other two. There was nothing the school could take away from them or deny them.

As unfair as that seemed to us, it was just as clear that we had a responsibility to turn all three in. We saw them. They knew we saw them. They all but flaunted it in our faces. We all knew the rule. To not report them was to make a mockery of all school rules and our ability to maintain order. But we all heard what Henry had said, too. And that, it seemed to Curt and I, made the results of reporting even more unfair. We were still discussing the pros and cons when the bus pulled up in front of the school about 9:00 P.M. that night.

I know a lot of you would like me to come down on the side of fairness on this one. But we didn't. Curt and I chose the law instead. We did so because it was the right thing to do, and we had known that all along. We knew there was a bigger picture to look at. There were principles, ethics, and honor involved. Not just for us and these three boys, but for teachers and students everywhere. We had only struggled so long because we were not happy with the inequity of what was to happen respectively to the three boys. And it even turned out worse than we thought. Back in those days, all glories a student earned during the year, including athletic letters, were bestowed upon each student at an awards day program on one of the last days of school. Not only did Harry miss the remainder of the baseball season, including play-offs, and did not get his baseball letter, but they did not give him the football letter he had earned months earlier. Talk about unfair.

But life is not fair. If it were millions of people would not be living in squalor around the world while we live a life of relative ease here in America. Life is not fair. No one ever promised us it would be. I'm not backing away from anything I've said before. I still absolutely believe that we all must accept full responsibility for our behavior. I hope Harry has forgiven me. I was doing my job as I saw it. And he knew what he had agreed to, and he knew he had broken the agreement and expected to be punished. I am truly sorry he was punished so severely. None of us foresaw that coming. I sincerely hope that Harry learned something of greater value than a high school letter.

"People know what they
do; they frequently
know why they do what
they do; but what they
don't know is what
what they do does."
—Michel Foucalt
The Order of Things

Chapter Thirty

I do not believe the consequences were fair to Harry. I'm glad the state high school league and the legislature has seen fit to change the guidelines so they are more equitable. I am equally glad the school does its very best to combat teenage alcohol, tobacco, and other illegal drug abuse. It is a very serious problem, folks. And it is not going away without the cooperation of the whole community.

While reading an article on student ineligibility a couple years ago in *The Paynesville Press,* I thought of the adage, "The more things change, the more they stay the same." Having seen variations on this theme my entire life. (I have been on all sides of this eligibility question at some point. I have been the student, the parent, most often, the school person), the similarites in each instance are clear to me. There are several observations I'd like to share. Feel free to take what fits for you and leave the rest.

The school, not unlike the police and others in authority, has the job of enforcing the rules as set forth by the school board, the State High School League, and the laws of our society. There are certain parameters within which the school is obliged to conduct its business. In every case with which I am familiar, schools have operated within those boundaries. Parents, on the other hand, often place their focus on protecting their children. Rightfully so, they seek to support and defend their children. They wish to see no harm come to them. They wish only good things and successful outcomes. Frequently, when parents and school authorities have different objectives, these two paths become a collision course.

The two sides tend to polarize. The battle lines get drawn. Tempers flare. Ugly things are said. Fingers are pointed. The name-calling starts. Blame is placed. Half-truths and lies are spoken. Each side fails to see the position of the other. None of these actions help solve the problem on either a short- or long-term basis. They, in fact, become part of the problem. And these behaviors stand in the way of the healing that is necessary following an incident. Sometimes unnecessary scars remain long after the flak has settled, and hurts are created from which communities never heal.

This is further complicated by the fact that our society has pretty much embarked upon an adversarial course of its own. The trend, for years, has been away from seeking truth and justice, and toward winning at whatever cost. Forget guilt or innocence. Forget right and wrong. Find the nearest loophole and jump right through. Our legal and political systems are classic examples. People have become far more interested in who wins than they are in what's right. I think we need to keep our focus on solutions, both long and short range, and we need to work together to find those answers. For his musical, *Into the Woods*, Stephen Sondheim wrote a beautiful song entitled "Children Will Listen." Part of the words are:

"Careful the things you say, children will listen.
Careful the things you do, children will see—and learn.
Children will look to you, for which way to turn—to learn what to be.
Careful before you say, "listen to me.""

All the wisdom I have read or wise people I have talked to have shared a belief that adversity helps us to grow as humans. I can't ever remember discussing the subject with anyone who hasn't shared his/her own story about a lesson learned from something that seemed, at the time, to be really bad. (The word growth has an "ow" right in the middle.) I believe we need to be very careful about the messages we are sending our children. We need to be certain that what we are protecting them from isn't denying them access to a larger and a more important life lesson—one that has greater staying power.

Finally I want to make a suggestion to the young folks who in the past, present, or future find themselves in this situation. The agreement you signed did not say, "I agree to try not getting caught drinking alcohol." Among other things, you agreed to not use alcohol and other drugs. You and your parents signed a contract. Your coaches are fully aware of the pledge you signed. Furthermore, the consequences for violating that agreement were explicitly spelled out to you before you signed. The first offense would carry a penalty of two weeks ineligibility. That penalty was not to be enforced at your convenience. The consequence was to be immediate.

You entered that contract with your eyes wide open. You knew what you were doing when you signed it. And you knew what you were doing when you broke it. Please, for your own sake, assume full responsiblity for your behavior. Not because of what the school says. Not because of what your parents say. But because it is the right thing to do. Do it for you.

That's where forgiveness and healing begin.

"Golf is an invitation
To ask your soul,
'Mind if I join you?'"
—Nike TV Commercial

Chapter Thirty-One

I have suggested in previous writings that golf is a microcosm of life, a position advanced by many about golf and other sports. I believe that to be basically true. Most of what we do, like most golf shots, is pretty average, but occasionally there is the spectacular and the awful. The ball does, in fact, go exactly where you hit it, and you have to play the ball where it lies. There is always a penalty for the trouble we get ourselves into, but there is a way out of the trouble too. And the more you respect the rules of the game, the more likely you are to find yourself in harmony with nature, other people, and yourself. But some recent sports viewing has shown me that golf is, in a very major way, not like life at all. IT IS BETTER!

In the American League Championship Series between the Yankees and the Orioles, a twelve-year-old boy reached over the barrier, the ball hit the heel of his glove and caromed into the stands. The umpire called it a home run. The Yankees won the game in extra innings and ultimately the right to play the Braves in the World Series. Arguably that game would have ended with the Orioles winning in nine innings; that may have changed the entire series. Conceivably, the outcome of the World Series may have been affected. Whether the boy is a hero or a villain is a matter of conjecture. My point here is that fan interference is common in baseball. In basketball, fans go to extreme measures to distract opponents attempting free throws. In soccer, they have been known to trample each other to death.

How many times have you seen a golf gallery deliberately interfere with an errant tee shot? They are more likely to stand there and get hit rather than purposely alter the ball's flight pattern. When have you witnessed golf fans cross the barrier, a measly thin yellow rope, to disturb a player? Would even the most ardent golf fanatic even consider snatching a ball from the rough as a souvenir? My wife and I watch a lot of TV golf and have been to a few tournaments, and we've yet to see anything that even resembles "fan interference." Where other sports fans are rude and boorish, most golf fans, mostly golfers themselves, are courteous and respectful of both players and the rules.

During a Monday night football game between the Packers and Forty-Niners a few years ago, a Green Bay receiver caught a pass, fell down, got up and scampered into the end zone. The referee signaled touchdown. The Forty-Niners hollered foul. Another official raised a question about the the call, and a conference was called. While the officials huddled, the Monday Night Football broadcasting crew analyzed several instant replay views. The first clearly showed that a defensive player had touched the receiver while he was on the ground. He should have been down at that point. Another view hinted that perhaps the the ball hadn't even been caught cleanly. Possibly it should have been ruled an incomplete pass. While the officials were discussing the various possibilities, did that wide receiver go over and reveal that a defender had touched him after he fell? Inconceivable! Right? Would he ever divulge the ball had hit the ground and bounced back into his hands? Of course not! Such disclosure is unheard of in other sports. Instead, players and teams feel they got away with one. One of the announcers actually said, "The Packers got away with one that time."

Okay. Fine. That's the nature of the game. There's big bucks involved. Championship trophies. How important was that decision? Well, the fourth quarter ended with a tie score, and Green Bay won the game in overtime. Had the initial decision been overturned the outcome might have been different. Maybe even who ulitmately got the home field advantage at playoff time. You certainly can't expect a player to make an honest disclosure with that much at stake. And it would be ridiculous to think that one of the other players would reveal the truth.

The day after that football game, however, I read where Mark Calcavecchia discovered he had erroneously signed a score card for the final round of the Texas Open. He already had a check in hand for $10,817. Did he smile to himself and say, "I got away with one?" No. He called the PGA and reported the error. He was disqualified from the tournament and forfieted his winnings. Why would he do such a thing? Simply because he is a golfer, and he knew it was the right thing to do. Golfers, at least on the golf course, do the right thing.

The following week a tour rookie, Taylor Smith, tied with Tiger Woods for the PGA Disney Classic Championship. The prize? $216,000. Even losing in a playoff would have netted him nearly $130,000. But his playing partner that day told an official he believed Smith's putter was illegal. Result? Disqualification. Bye-bye to the two-hundred sixteen grand or even cab fare to the airport. Was he furious at his playing partner? His exact words were, "Lennie (Clements) did the right thing. He had to protect the field."

Since I brought up Woods, let's make another kind of comparison. Travis Lee, the top-rated baseball player in the 1996 draft was given ten-million dollars in salary, bonuses and incentives to play baseball. He was guaranteed a major league contract for his first professional season. This was based on his potential, which is considerable. He has produced precious little as a ball player so far.

Woods, possibly the top-rated amateur golfer of all time decided to turn professional after winning his third consecutive U.S. Amateur Championship. Instead of being given bonuses or guarantees, he had to earn his 1997 PGA card by finishing among the top 125 players in 1996. And there were only seven tournaments left in which to do so. The fact that he did it in grand style is irrelevant here. (For all of you who thought *Tin Cup* was unbelievable, consider Tiger's true tale.)

Golfers are paid according to how well they play each week. Other sports pay huge salaries based on either potential or past performance. What Phil Mikkelson makes in the next seven years will be determined by how his scores compare with all the other golfers in each and every tournament. The Los Angeles Lakers, on the other hand, will shell out 120-million dollars during that span to Shaquille O'Neal no matter how well or poorly he plays basketball in any given game or season. It will not matter whether the Lakers win or lose. If other players outscore or out rebound him, it's okay. Others will undoubtedly block more shots and have more assists. Certainly others will make more free throws. No problem for Shaq. He signed a contract, based on his enormous potential, and he will be paid that amount. Period.

These comparisons, by the way, do not consider corporate sponsorships. That is a whole other matter. How much Nike, Titleist, or Pepsi is willing to throw at a sports hero is about the corporation and its values (and ours as a society) not about the athlete or the sport.

Athletes in other sports complain about playing time. Golfers play if they prove themselves good enough. They have to make the cut in each tournament. Coaches, managers, and players argue with and even abuse officials. Do Roberto Alomar or Albert Bell come to mind? Golfers accept the decisions of the officials even when that ruling is over a technicality and/or an interpretation of a nit-picking rule. I could venture outside the sports arena and make comparisons with the rude and obnoxious behavior we find in all walks of life. And I'm sure golfers everywhere are guilty of as much as anyone else. I know I am.

But at least the game itself as it is played by both the most frustrated hacker and the consummate professional is not merely a game that mirrors life. It transcends it. Golf is played in a parallel universe—a higher plane. Between the first tee and the eighteenth green lies a better world. A world that, in many ways, makes more sense. A world that is much closer to the civility with which we were intended to live our lives. A Nike television commercial in 1996 sums it up nicely.

> "Golf is an invitation
> To feel the grass,
> To hear the trees.
> Golf is an invitation
> To play well and know
> it's going to end;
> To play poorly and think
> it's never going to end.
> Golf is an invitation
> To know God,
> To know Satan,
> To ignore fear,
> To be Nick Price.
> Golf is an invitation
> To ask your soul,
> "Mind if I join you?"
> Golf is an invitation.
> You are invited."

Golf is not merely a microcosm of life. IT IS BETTER!

Chapter Thirty-Two

Following is an essay I wrote in March of 1974 that was printed in *The Paynesville Press*. It is titled "The Night I Understood What High School Athletics Is All About." I'm including it here for a couple reasons. First of all, I like it and I think it still has merit after a quarter century. Secondly, it leads into some comments I wish to write about the condition of sports in America today. Here's the essay:

It wasn't a big, earth-shattering revelation. It wasn't anything I didn't know before. As a matter of fact, I wasn't even there when it happened, and I can't adequately tell you what it is now. But, in one lingering moment of a basketball game, the whole purpose of high school athletics crystallized in my mind.

I had been sick and decided to stay home. By the time I got the radio on, it was nearly half-time and we (Paynesville High School) were down by a score of thirty to twenty-one. We managed to pull within one point before the buzzer ended the half. I listened as the announcer reviewed the scoring. I realized that (Dave) Hedlund wasn't playing. Dave, who is not a superstar but he has been our starting center for three years, is a good ballplayer and vital to the team.

For two days, the anxiety in school centered around whether or not his injury would keep him out of the game. It had and our hopes seemed slim without him.

The twenty two-minutes that followed is the lingering moment of basketball action I referred to earlier. Before regulation time ended, a starting guard had fouled out—but the buzzer sounded with the score tied. In the first overtime, we lost our best rebounder and our top scorer. That period ended in a tie. We started the second overtime with three sophomores who had been on the "B" squad when the season started, a junior who had seen little action during the season, and one regular guard. That last regular fouled out and was replaced by a senior who had missed half the season with a broken foot. The deck had been stacked against us at the outset, and fate had been dealing from the bottom all night. And we won the game! And it didn't surprise me that we did.

I wasn't surprised because, throughout that second half, I kept recalling watching these kids perform in Paynesville athletics since last May when several players were ready to write off 1973-1974 athletics.

My mind was flooded with vivid memories. I remembered eighth graders pressed into service as varsity baseball players, and I saw some of them get hits that helped win a few ball games. I remember a depleted track and field team perform almost superhumanly in a valiant effort to win one more conference crown for a retiring coach. Not one regular returned for cross country, but I saw freshmen on stubby legs fight doggedly over the golf course hills to salvage a measure of respect in that sport. I remembered an injury and ineligibility riddled football team fighting toe-to-toe with some of the toughest teams in the area. Inexperienced wrestlers found themselves forced into varsity jobs unexpectedly, and they performed far beyond anyone's expectations.

What these memories brought into sharp focus for me is important in understanding athletic competition. In this time, I haven't seen a Paynesville athlete give less than the full-measure of his ability. I haven't seen a team fold under pressure. I haven't heard these students complain, make excuses, or ask for special consideration because they got some bad breaks. I've seen the Paynesville athletes shoulder their responsibilities with pride and dignity.

We haven't won a conference championship. Our won-lost record is below what we have been accustomed to in past seasons. But, in my opinion, this has been the most successful sports season we have had since I came. I can honestly say I've seen boys turned into men. And that is what high school athletics is all about. And I'm deeply grateful that we have an administration and a coaching staff that recognizes it.

Chapter Thirty-Three

I have been a sports fan for as long as I can remember. My dad, my grandpa Perry, my uncle Art, and my brother, Jack, helped foster in me a love for sports and a deep appreciation for those who play the games with both skill and honor. My early heroes were all athletes—mostly baseball players like Stan Musial, Ted Williams, Jackie Robinson, and Joe DiMaggio. There were football players, too. There was Doc Blanchard and Glen Davis from Army and Doak Walker from SMU. Boxing was a big thing in my family, so Joe Louis, Sugar Ray Robinson, and Rocky Graziano were childhood idols, too. And I loved the local athletes. High school stars like Chuck Wolfe and college stars like Wes Luther. The Minot Mallards semi-pro baseball team had some special players, too, "Zoonie" McLean and "Sugar" Cain were my favorites. One of my greatest thrills was watching Satchel Paige pitch against those Mallards.

I loved sports.

I spent hours bouncing a baseball off the front steps of my house. If I hit the steps one way, I would get a hot grounder back at my feet. If my throw would catch the corner of a step, the result was a fly ball or pop up. I would play

135

nine inning games all by myself. Jack and I played one-on-one football games in our back yard, and we boxed in our basement. I shot hoops in our driveway on a regular basis. On rainy days and at night, I played sports board games like All-Star Baseball or one of two football games I owned; one had a vibrating field where you absolutely could not control the direction players moved, while the other had a lighted window that revealed the result of the play you selected. I even made up games for the three major sports using the plastic soldier and cowboy figures you bought at the dime store. Every month I read *Sport* magazine from cover to cover.

I lived sports.

Fast forward now. The last couple years, we've been hearing the Twins may leave Minnesota. They can't compete with the big money market cities unless they get a new stadium. The Vikings are whining the same tune. There is a lack of interest on the part of the fans; we won't support new stadiums. Before Randy Moss injected some adrenalin into the Vikings predictable offense, we were experiencing games being blacked out on local television because these games weren't sold out.

Sports columnists are puzzled. Dark Starr, on WCCO, is asking why.

What is wrong for Pete's sake? Minneapolis is a great sports city.

I can't speak for a lot of folks but, in brief, here's my story.

I don't really care that much anymore.

I became a St. Louis Cardinal fan the day before my eleventh birthday. It was October 15, 1946, when Enos "Country" Slaughter, broken elbow and all, scored from first base on a single by Harry Walker to win the World Series for the Redbirds. That single play embodied everything I had been taught about how to play the game. Slaughter was injured, but he was willing to play hurt because the team needed him in the lineup. I'm not so sure now that playing hurt was always the wisest thing to do, but it sure is easier to admire than some of today's pampered stars who sit out with a hangnail or a bad hair day. On that play, Slaughter gave everything he had. Everything. He took the Red Sox by surprise when he charged around third and headed for home. It was a great play. A great strategy. It beat waiting around for one of the sluggers to hit a home run so he could stroll home. So I became a Cardinal fan and, as late as 1987, was one of the few Minnesotans rooting for them to beat the Twins in that World Series.

As a youngster, I was a Gopher football fan who would sit faithfully by the radio each and every fall Saturday to listen to the heroics of Billy Bye, Bud Grant, Paul Giel, and Bob McNamara. Whitey Skoog was a basketball hero of mine as were all the other Gophers who played from the late forties into the nineties. I was a fan of the Flanagan brothers and other professional boxers from Minnesota. I was ecstatic when the Twins moved to Minnesota and even more so when the Vikings arrived. I was a huge fan. Anything that happened in baseball, football, basketball, or boxing interested me. I read the *Star Tribune* sports page religiously (I loved the peach section when I was a kid). I subscribed to *Sport, Sports Illustrated*, and *The Sporting News.*

I still admit an allegiance to college basketball and some interest in the Vikings; I watch them on most Sundays because I don't have much else to do. I give the sports page a cursory glance every morning, read no sports magazines regularly, except *Golf*, and I really don't care if the Twins, the Vikings, or both leave the state. I prefer they both stay. I think they bring something to the state and attract visitors who, in turn, spend money on hotels, restaurants and bars, casinos, and shopping malls. Their economic impact is probably greater than most of us are aware. But I want them to be honest. Don't try to tell me the new ballpark and stadium is for the benefit of the average fan. Nothing in sport today is done for the fans' benefit. They want the big corporate boxes and the guaranteed money that comes with that. Old Met stadium had the average fan in mind.

My lack of interest is primarily due to what has happened to sport franchises in recent years. There is, in my opinion, nothing to be loyal to. And teams have no one to blame but themselves if the fans lack interest. The teams, players and management, lost their interest in me long before I finally, out of frustration, lost interest in them.

When I followed those early Cardinals, I could count on Musial, Schoendienst, Kurowski, and Slaughter to be in the lineup every day. I knew Harry Brecheen would be ready to pitch every fourth day. In later years, I knew I could count on Lou Brock, Curt Flood, and Bob Gibson. They were givens. When those teams of the fifties played the Dodgers, they would face Snider, Robinson, Furillo, Reese, and Hodges. More givens. Sure there were occasional trades and roster changes, but the line-ups remained pretty consistent. In other words, the Cardinals were the Cardinals. The Dodgers were the Dodgers, and the Yankees were the Yankees. Remember the 1991 Twins who thrilled us so with their remarkable last-to-first pennant drive and subsequent World Series victory? Where was the heroic winning pitcher, local boy, Jack Morris, just one year later? How about Chuck Knoblach, who left a few years later because he "wanted to be on a winning team." For Chuck, a clue seems to be optional. Ted Willaims and Ernie Banks are but two hall-of-famers who toiled their entire illustrious careers for teams that never won a pennant.

You see, there is no Minnesota Twins anymore (or Vikings or anyone else). There are twenty-five guys who don a Twins uniform for 162 games a year, but when there contract is up, they sell out to the highest bidder. Or the owners dump the players if they don't fit under the salary cap or are otherwise deemed expendable or unaffordable. Players aren't loyal to the team. Teams aren't loyal to the players. Neither seems to give a hoot about the fans. It's all about money and/or ego, and I, for one, have had all I care for.

I'll stick to hacking around Koronis Hills Golf Course.

Chapter Thirty-Four

I saw it in an art gallery/shop in Sedona, Arizona. I was awe struck. I've always considered myself an art fancier of sorts—not a connoisseur by any means because I don't understand the nuances and intricacies of fine art. But when I see something I really like, it usually mesmerizes me. At least for a while. I can become totally drawn into a piece of art. I find myself both admiring the talents of the artist and thoroughly enjoying the story being told by the *objet d' art.*

In sixty years, many such pieces have crossed my path. Never has one stopped me as this sculpture in Sedona did. While my wife, Mary, my daughter, Jodi, and granddaughter, Megan, browsed various parts of the store, I leisurely wandered around hoping something would catch my eye. Then I saw the sculpture. It stopped me dead in my tracks. I don't even remember for sure, but I think it was bronze. I do remember it as awesome. It was a wonderful story sitting on a podium.

It was called *The Gathering Storm* or *The Coming Storm* or something about a storm. By now, you are fully aware that not only the nuances and intricacies escape me, but some pretty broad strokes too. I'll give you that. Just the other day Mary said to me, jokingly, "Boy, I can't get anything past you can I?"

"Honey," I answered, "you could probably get the Goodyear blimp past me." But I digress.

I stopped and stared at this marvelous piece of work for who knows how long. I was totally absorbed in the tale it was spinning. It was an ineffable moment with time standing still. There before me were five figures on either side of a door. On the outside was a small family—husband, wife, and an infant. Inside a mother and child. As I drank in this scene, I was certain someone was going to get hurt. Quite possibly killed.

The three on the outside were Native Americans. They were wrapped in heavy skins and blankets to protect themselves from the cold. The baby was barely visible as the parents had him bundled tightly to keep away the cold and the bone-chilling wind suggested by the billowing blankets and clothing. Their grimaces were further evidence of the frigid conditions. It was very obvious this young couple was desperate to protect their baby from the storm. They had to get inside.

The woman on the other side of the door had a single focus too—to protect her child. Her facial expression was one of terror. Her head was, no doubt, filled with horror stories of white women being raped and murdered on these prairies by the "savages" whose land they were occupying. As unfair as these prejudices may be, they leap to mind in moments of stress and confusion. We tend to panic. We don't always do the right thing. Basic instincts overtake us.

And this woman's instinct was to protect her child at all costs. The door is latched. She has a rifle. And she will, by God, protect her child. She may, in quieter times, know the right thing to do. The loving thing. At this moment, the look on her face says she's scared. And fear is the antithesis of love. Her fear motivates her to protect her child.

A sales clerk who had noticed my interest in the piece came over to talk with me about it. Mary, Jodi, and Megan soon joined us. The clerk, a Native herself, asked what I thought would happen. I shared my pessimism. I told her someone was going to die or, at the very least, be seriously hurt. She was surprised. The others are too. Frankly so was I. At myself. I don't often take such a dim view. The clerk said, "I think she will let them in." Everyone agreed.

Except me.

And I want to. I want these ladies to be right. I want so badly to be wrong. I pray I am wrong. I'm a loving and compassionate man. I see myself as relatively free from racial prejudices. But I think I have some understanding of people, and I know our history. I know that ninety percent of the Native population was wiped out between the arrival of Columbus and Wounded Knee. They died at the hands of the white man.

I want that pioneer woman to open the door and invite that native family to share the warmth of her fire. I want the clerk and my family to be right. But my perceptions keep telling me that the young brave, driven by his protective instincts, is more likely to bust that door latch, rush into the room, and be met by the pioneer lady's knee-jerk reaction to fire the rifle. And somebody will end up hurt. Or dead.

There are other scenarios, of course. And we will never know. These figures are frozen on that pedestal allowing each of us to draw our own conclusions. That's what great art does. In this case, my heart lead me one way. History the other.

There was another statue that caught my eye that day. It showed a couple men rowing a fishing boat in a very turbulent sea. The men were fighting mightily to keep the boat afloat. They were losing. The sculptor froze them in time and space with the boat angled about eighty degrees out of the water. The bow was pointed skyward, and they were about to capsize. The piece was called *Sockdolager*. An appropriate name. Sockdolager is defined by Webster's as "the final or decisive blow; the finisher."

Isn't that a wonderfully descriptive word? I love words like this. One single word that captures an entire moment or concept. No need to waste a lot of other words to explain the dire consequences these seamen were facing. Why continue with a lengthy description of their peril when that single word—sockdolager—says it all?

Sockdolager!

The finisher.

Game over.

"It doesn't require
many words
to speak the truth."
—Chief Joseph

Chapter Thirty-Five

Words fascinate me. Especially words like "sock-dolager." Colorful words that dance around your tongue before they spill out like symphonies. Every language is loaded with such words. One of my favorite English words is "serendipity." Say it aloud: Serendipity. Isn't that fun to say? There is a lilt to it that few words can claim. And the meaning? Ah, the meaning is even better. Serendipity means sudden, unexpected good fortune—especially when something in which you feared the worst provides an unexpected gift. What a spectacular concept wrapped up in that spectacular word. We have all had those serendipitous moments.

They can be as routine as a phone call on a dreary day from someone you never expected to hear from again or while grudgingly cleaning the attic you happen upon an old photograph that takes you into a two-hour reverie from a cherished moment from your halcyon days. And they can be life-changing experiences like meeting a future spouse while attending the funeral of a dear friend. When I applied for graduate school, I had to drive seventy-five miles in heavy snow to take the Miller Analogies Test. The test lasted from

143

8:00 A.M. until noon. The snow intensified. The test was difficult. The test was impossible. The snow continued.

With each successive question, I was more sure I was failing. I felt like an idiot by the time twelve o'clock rolled around. And I stepped out into a raging blizzard. I couldn't even consider driving home. I was short of cash, so I checked into the cheapest hotel in town and spent the rest of the day and night wallowing in misery and self-pity, contemplating what a dumbbell I was. I was convinced I had blown my chances of ever getting into grad school. The storm worsened, and I knew that even God was against me. I felt lonely, depressed, AND STUPID.

And I pretty much stayed that way until later in the week when I got my acceptance letter. Gloom to elation in seven seconds. Serendipity. A similar word in Sanskrit is *raudrananda*—the conversion of pain into pleasure. *Raudrananda* sort of tickles the tongue, too, doesn't it? If the seas in the *Sockdolager* scuplture suddenly calmed it would certainly be *raudrananda*. The Portuguese have a word, *saudade*, which means pain and pleasure at the same time, but you'd better get a masochist to explain that to you.

Perhaps to understand what I'm driving at here, you need to possess *shoshin*. *Shoshin* is what the Japanese call a beginner's mind. Take special note of the term beginner. We are speaking here of a totally open and ready mind. A beginner's mind is one that is ready for anything and open to everything. It is a mind of many possibilities. There is no prejudgment or expectation. Reading this paragraph illustrates that the English language requires lengthy explanation to convey this idea. In Japan, one succinct word—*shoshin*—says it all.

With *shoshin* maybe we could finally solve some of the human problems with which we have struggled forever. By ridding our selves of preconceived notions and starting with *shoshin,* we just might attain *aroha.* This a Maori term that embraces the all-encompassing quality of goodness expressing love for the people, land, birds, animals, fish, plants, and all living things. It is a one-word recognition of the interconnectedness of all life. A song when you pronounce it, *aroha* is a small word that carries a huge load on its shoulders. A person who has *aroha* expresses genuine concern for others and acts with their best interests in mind. *Aroha,* to the Maori, is not merely a word or concept. It is a way of doing and being. If you have *aroha,* you would probably have achieved *ahisma.* In Sanskrit this is considered the natural condition of the human spirit, a state in which no violence—neither thought nor action—exists.

To possess the quality of *aroha,* one must practice *okolakicye,* a Lakota word that is a fellowship necessary for unity. This beautiful indigenous word adds to my mix the message that we can't do it alone. It requires the fellowship of many. We must work together to achieve the best for ourselves and others. "Live with a purpose and concern for the people." wrote Phil Lane, Jr., a Yankton Lakota elder, "Its [life] is brief, my friends."

Once you have achieved *aroha* and put *okolakicye* to use in your everyday living, you just might be able to understand *kukaroo.* This is a lousy segue but bear with me; it just might be worth the trip. Like most of the other words, I'm not exactly sure how to pronounce this Micronesian word, but it is a most favorite concept of mine. No matter how you say it, it is bound to come out sounding playful. As it should because it describes the delightfully blissful state of doing nothing. On purpose. I love it when I can go *kukaroo*: to just hang out, relaxing—just being. It doesn't equate with laziness, idleness, or sloth. It's about just BEING. My God, what a feeling. Enjoying being you for no particular reason. Achievement or accomplishment isn't important when you go *kukaroo.* Do you see the beauty of this word? This concept? I feel compelled to explain and then explain the explanation to be sure I'm not misunderstood. The Micronesians simply say, "I'm going *kukaroo.*"

None of these ideas is easy to grasp. Oh, we may intellectually understand them, but to truly "get it" deep in your bones you probably have had to pass a stage of life the Ojibwe call *mizaanatigwan.* That's a real mouthful, and if you want a correct pronunciation you better find an Ojibwe elder. He or she would not only pronounce it correctly but would explain it much better than I can. I understand it to mean the first forty years is the rough road. I'm not sure that forty is carved in stone, but I am quite certain that it means you have survived the worst. You have met all the challenges presented you, have learned and grown through those experiences, and are now ready to enjoy the benefits and rewards you have earned.

I don't know if the Ojibwe have a word for what comes after *mizaanatigwan,* but the Indonesians do—*belum. Belum* simply means the best is yet to come, probably implied in *mizaanatigwan.* Again I am awe struck that so much can be said with a single word. Sort of makes me wonder why most of us talk so damn much. We are, as a matter of fact, quite skilled at using a whole lot of words to say relatively little. Mary thinks it's one of my best qualities.

Perhaps no single word in any language expresses so much as the Polynesian (Hawaiian) word *aloha.* In context it may mean one of several things—hello, goodbye, love—it's sort of the yin/yang of words. But no wonder it's such a potent word. I saw it broken down as *alo*—the bosom of the universe and *ha*—the breath of God. Nothing could possibly be more all-encompassing than a word that literally translates as God breathing life into the entire universe. That's a mighty big concept for a simple five letter word.

Now I have arrived at my very favorite word in any language. We are all familiar with the image of two East Indians greeting each other with heads bowed and hands folded, prayer-like, at chest level. The oral greeting that accompanies this picture is *namaste.* The word personalizes the concepts embraced by *aloha.* Namaste means "I honor the divine in you." Wow! How the world would change if *namaste* were the "in your bones" belief of each of us. Our goal in all relationships would be for the divine spirit in us to connect with the divine spirit in ALL those you encounter—spouses, children, bosses and co-workers, store clerks, custodians, strangers in town—everyone.

That's a hope I have when I write. I don't ever expect readers to agree with all my ideas. I don't even expect they will always make sense. But I always hope that something of my spirit will connect with the reader's spirit and create a bond—a sense of *aroha, namaste,* and/or *okolakicye.*

I'll end this word play with yet another fabulous concept in a word (actually a phrase this time)—*mi taku oyasin,* the phrase with which the Lakota people end their prayers. Literal translation: all my relations. Since their belief is that we all—red, white, black, and yellow—are kinfolk, the intention is a blessing for all people on the planet.

May you and all your relations experience *kukaroo, aroha,* and all the concepts expressed in these wonderful words.

> "The whole world had
> changed.
> Only the fairy tales
> remained the same."
> —*Number the Stars*
> Lois Lowry

Chapter Thirty-Six

Children's books have always been, for me, sources of great wisdom. While entertaining children, authors have been sneaking the great truths of the world into the minds of the adults who read them—and, hopefully, planting these seeds in the bones of the young listeners and readers. From the moment I started this book, I had planned to include a chapter on children's literature. I got a little nudge from Amy Gash, another lover of the genre who has published a beautiful book of quotations, *What the Dormouse Said*, subtitled "Lessons for Grown-Ups from Children's Books."

Her work contains hundreds of treasured lines she discovered as she read to her son. "I'm convinced," she wrote, "that children's authors are often the neglected giants of literature." She has neatly cataloged her favorites into such categories as imagination, friendship, family, nature, reverence, and several other essential to life areas. As a result her book serves as a handy primer for living. I wish I had thought of such a book. I'll have to be content muddling along in my own haphazard style.

I want to share some of my favorite thoughts gleaned from those children's books I have cherished and perhaps

I'll include a few that, thanks to Amy Gash, are from books I am now looking forward to reading. (I'll steal material from my friends, but I have enough ethics to credit strangers for what they contribute to my writings, speeches, humor, and wisdom.)

Few of us alive today would accomplish much or undertake difficult tasks if it weren't for Watty Piper. Watty wrote a children's classic back in 1930 that has been an inspiration to nearly every child at some point or another. There have been scores of printings of his little jewel, and I'm sure it has been translated into most languages. And yet, I'd be surprised if you know, at this point, who Watty Piper is or what he wrote. I'd be even more surprised if you haven't chanted or at least thought "I think I can, I think I can" when faced with a most difficult challenge. Mr. Piper wrote *The Little Engine That Could* over seventy years ago, and children ever since have identified with that little steam engine's pluck and determination. Who knows how far-reaching those magic words have been? Perhaps they spurred on a young Jonas Salk or Bill Gates. Maybe Oprah. Steven Spielberg?

I know my mom read it to me, and I've shared it with both my children and grandchildren. I'm sure I never consciously thought about those words when I faced some daunting task or impossible dream but the concept was firmly etched in some neural pathway in my brain.

Thanks, Watty.

The cornerstone of my counseling career surely was placed back when I first heard/saw/read *Alice in Wonderland*. There's a scene where Alice has angered the Queen of Hearts who has just ordered Alice's head chopped off. I told you she was angry. Alice, who is precocious but not stupid, runs for her life followed by the queen's henchmen brandishing swords and the Queen who kept shouting, "Off with her head!" Alice comes upon a place where the road forks in several directions. She stops and confusedly looks at the many choices. At that point, the Cheshire Cat appears.

"Could you tell me, please," asked Alice, "which way I should go?"

"That all depends a good deal," replied the cat, "on where you want to get to."

Since, at that particular moment, she had more urgent thoughts, Alice told him, rather emphatically, "I don't much care where."

The Cheshire Puss paused, looking disdainfully at the poor creature below. "Then it would seem, " he said smugly, "it doesn't really matter which way you go."

That sums up for me the essence of counseling. None of my college professors or textbooks had ever made it that clear. Whatever a client is dealing with—college choice, suicide, drug use, career moves, divorce of parents, classes to take, relationships, grief—if he or she doesn't care where they end up, the path they choose doesn't really matter. If, on the other hand, he or she does care how things turn out, it matters a great deal which choices he or she makes. Some roads are aimed at a healthy, productive, happy life while other paths will make it extremely difficult to reach those, or any other, goals. As Dr. Suess so aptly puts it in *Oh, The Places You'll Go*. "You have brains in your head. You have feet in your shoes. You can steer yourself any direction you choose."

My very favorite children's book is *Hope For the Flowers*. It was written and illustrated by Trina Paulus, and it is the story of two caterpillars, Stripe and Yellow, who meet as they struggle to reach the top of a "caterpillar pillar." Once they make personal contact, the pillar doesn't seem important, and they abandon the climb and make a life for themselves on the ground. Stripe, the male, grows restless and decides he has to know the secret of the top. He resumes the climb, and Yellow, his mate, wanders off unsure of life's purpose but knowing she won't find it back on the pillar. She meets an old caterpillar spinning a cocoon. After he explains what he's doing, she asks how one becomes a butterfly.

His answer is an axiom for us all. "You must want to fly so much that you're willing to give up being a caterpillar."

While Yellow risks becoming a butterfly, Stripe ruthlessly pushes his way nearly to the top only to discover that for anyone to reach the top those already there have to be pushed off. Yellow has made her transformation and flies to show Stripe. He starts down. Again. This time he knows it's the right choice, and he excitedly tells fellow crawlers, "We can fly! We can become butterflies! There's nothing at the top, and it doesn't matter."

That sums up my feelings on the rat race and grind we've created. Our technology and thirst for power have outdistanced our humanity and spirituality, and I think we need to take a look at our "pillar" and realize the rewards "at the top" are pretty shallow. We need a lot less show and a lot more substance.

Children's literature deals with death every bit as effectively as it does life. If you are having trouble explaining death to your youngster—or your grandmother, for that matter—share Leo Buscaglia's *The Fall of Freddie the Leaf* with her. Freddie is the last leaf on an oak tree as fall winds its way toward winter. Unable to hang on any longer, Freddie finally lets go and tumbles to earth. "Freddie landed on the snow, not knowing spring would follow and plans for new leaves were asleep in the ground." The last page simply says "THE BEGINNING."

As James Barrie reminds us in *Peter Pan*, "To die will be an awfully big adventure." For a deeper understanding, try *There's No Such Place as Far Away* by my favorite author, Richard Bach. As birds and animals scurry to Rae's birthday party, the hummingbird asks, "Can miles truly separate you from friends? If you want to be with Rae (someone you love) aren't you already there?"

Can miles or death (or anything in the time-space continuum) truly separate us from friends? Amy Gash cited *Walk Two Moons* by Sharon Creech: "Sometime you know in your heart you love someone, but you have to go away before your head can figure it out."

Authors of children's books touch on every aspect of life. Laura Huxley in *Oneadayreason to be Happy* has Karen, the hero of her delightful tale, tell the dolphin she'd been riding, "I'm happy because I am!" You can give that sentence four or five meanings depending upon where you put the emphasis. Each, however, conveys an acceptance of self—flaws and all. Isn't that what Frank Baum wants us to glean from the wizard's wonderful self-assessment in *The Wonderful Wizard of Oz*: "I'm really a very good man, but I'm a very bad wizard." Elzie Segar and Bud Sagendorf, creators of that beloved cartoon character, Popeye, have the old sea dog express it this way: "I yam what I yam, an' tha's all that I yam."

And I hope, on one of my bad days, when I'm obsessing about a mistake I've made or can't let go of a character flaw, I remember Amy Tan's words from *The Moon Lady*. "How I loved my shadow, this dark side of me that loved all the things that no one else could see."

Everyone should read Canadian Robert Munsch. He eases occasional tension for us all in *Good Families Don't* in which he concludes, "good children do have farts, after all." In *The Paper Bag Princess*, Elizabeth, the heroine, outwits the dragon and saves the prince only to be told by him that she looks terrible with her hair tangled and wearing a dirty old paper bag and that she should return when "dressed like a real princess." Unlike so many girls in these types of stories, Elizabeth understood what really matters. She tells the Prince, "Your clothes are really pretty and your hair is very neat. You look like a real prince, but you are a bum." And she walked away to be perfectly happy without him. Munsch speaks for all mothers in *Love You Forever* when the mother in the story tells her son—from infancy through adulthood:

> "I'll love you forever,
> I'll like you for always,
> As long as I'm living
> my baby you'll be."

What all of these masters seem to know about is being real. Margery Williams, in *The Velveteen Rabbit*, says it, arguably, the best of all. "'Real isn't how you are made,' said the Skin Horse. 'It's a thing that happens to you. When a child loves you for a long time, not just to play with, but really loves you, then you become real."

'Does it hurt?' asked the Rabbit.

'Sometimes,' for he was always truthful, 'When you are real, you don't mind being hurt.'"

There's no end to the wisdom found in the books we share with our children and grandchildren from nursery rhymes to Harry Potter. How can you argue with Antoine de Saint Exupery whose *Little Prince* tells us, "It is only with the heart that one can see rightly; what is essential is invisible to the eye." (My personal favorite quote.)

Another of the wonderful messages for us in Lewis Carroll's wonderful *Alice in Wonderland* is Alice's response to the statement, "Oh, 'tis love, 'tis love that makes the world go round!"

Alice whispered, "That is done by everybody minding their own business. Ah well! It means much the same thing."

In *Where Have All the Children Gone,* Karen Kaiser Clarke explores the anxieties inherent in growing up. The little girl decides that patience is important. "It takes a lot of slow to grow," she explains. She finally accepts that she has no choice but to grow up. She hopes when it happens "I'll be some of the today me . . . I hope I'll grow deep and not just tall."

I highly recommend the books of Shel Silverstein, *Crow and Weasel* by Barry Lopez, *Old Turtle* by Doug Wood, Roald Dahl's *James and the Giant Peach*, and anything by Dr. Seuss. You can't help but learn something if you read children's literature. That's where you can tap into the child— the magic—that's still alive in you. "The sun is shining—the sun is shining. That's the magic. The flowers are growing— the roots are stirring. That is the magic. Being alive is the magic—being strong is the magic. The Magic is in me—the Magic is in me . . . . It's in every one of us." So spoke Francis Hodgson Burnett in *The Secret Garden*.

Chapter Thirty-Seven

I always wanted to be a little kid when I grew up. What a wonderful goal. My first encounter with that thought was in 1977 when I was taking a course at the Johnson Institute in Minneapolis. One of the class members had a t-shirt with those words printed on the back. It caught my attention then, and it has held it for twenty-three years. It has been a pretty compelling force in the latter part of my life. My actual childhood, as I have earlier written, was not the happiest (it was far from the worst) and not all of my memories are good ones.

One of the ways I learned to compensate was being hyper-vigilant. I assumed everything as my responsibility, except for the chores I disliked. When you take this stance, it is also natural to assume that when things go wrong it is your fault. If my parents argued, it was my fault. When my little sister got sick, it was my fault. If my dad got drunk, it was my fault. When my brother got in trouble, it was my fault. When the Korean War broke out in 1950 I heard the news on the radio and thought, "My God, what did I do now!"

I didn't allow myself a childhood. I took care of my sister. I got a job delivering papers when I was twelve. I went to

154

work for my dad at thirteen. Boy, was I grown up then. To prove it, I started to smoke. Later to drink. (Why is it when kids want to prove how grown up they are, they choose the most immature adult behaviors to mimic?) I certainly am not alone in that I never really had a childhood. So many of us were taught that we needed to grow up and stop acting foolish—as if those two were mutually exclusive. We worry so much about what others will think, oblivious to the obvious fact that most people don't pay that much attention. We immobilize ourselves with fear and stifle our natural child-like instincts, needs, and desires.

I'm not talking about being childish. Childish is, to me, when there's a huge communication gap within yourself—your head, your heart, and your behavior are not aligned. You're not in harmony. What I want is to be more child-like. So, what is a child like? A child is in awe of the world. They are great seekers. They can't wait to discover and unravel the great mysteries and wonders of this world. They love adventure. Children are alert. That probably explains why the babe who can barely sit up will spy the most minute article on the floor. Their great curiosity is why they have to taste it. If I could live my life over, I don't think I'd want to change a thing, but I would like to pay closer attention.

Children have a reverence for all creation. A child gives unconditional love better than anyone else. They meet another child on the playground, and there's an instant acceptance. They could care less about social or economic status. It matters not to them what color the other child's skin is or what church affiliation they have. They give no thought about whether the other can shoot hoops or is an honor student or the class clown. There are no barriers. They just don't care. They simply invite the other to swing or play on the monkey bars. There is a complete trust their new friend will love them back and not hurt them.

Children are playful. They laugh a lot. They giggle. They are able to find humor and joy in almost anything. And there's nothing hurtful in their humor. They don't have to cut another down to feel better about themselves. Their

155

humor is never at another's expense. The laughter of children is universally uplifting. The sounds of children playing and laughing brings out the best in us. The innocence and optimism of children is one of the greatest symbols of beauty and hope in the world. Small children are never bored. They know how to entertain themselves, aided by a vivid imagination that allows them to go anywhere or be anything they choose. They believe in the magical and mystical. Their world can include unicorns and dragons, gnomes and fairy godmothers, and red shoes that can take you back home again. They have imaginary friends and their stuffed animals and dolls are as real to them as anything. They have huge dreams.

Children haven't learned to stuff their feelings because they see no need for that. They allow themselves to get really excited. They jump up and down and clap their hands at surprises. They anticipate Christmas and birthdays in unbridled ways. They hug harder than adults. And when they are hurt, they allow the tears to flow freely without fear of embarrassment. No feelings are stifled. And they ask for what they need. When sad or lonely, they will crawl up in your lap and let you know they need to be held. If they have a "boo-boo," they ask you to kiss it and make it better. They are blatantly honest about what they need and freely express whatever feelings come as a result having those needs met or not.

For twenty-three years, I've been trying to be more like that. And I've had a lot of help. The people I've met in my recovery have been terrific in this area. In my first group experience with Partners in Prevention (PIP), my group facilitator, Dave Buker, opened my eyes to this issue and encouraged me to "let the kid out" in my personality. At first I took that to mean I could be really silly, but I have learned that it is much more than that. Other folks at PIP have helped me "grow down" too. My dear friend, Barb Elseth, gave me a birthday present, a "Certificate of the Right to Play," which hangs on the wall of my office. It grants me lifetime membership in The Society of Child-like Grownups, which forever bestows upon me the right to, among other things, "walk in the rain, build sand castles, dance, climb trees, ask lots of questions, learn new stuff, get excited, be a clown, and trust the universe." In big letters at the bottom, it reminds me "It's Never Too Late To Have A Happy Childhood."

I want to conclude this with a little piece my son Mark sent me via E-mail.

> To whom it may concern:
>
> I am hereby officially tendering my resignation as an adult.
>
> I have decided I would like to accept the responsibilities of an eight-year old again. I want to go to McDonald's and think it's a four-star restaurant. I want to sail sticks across a fresh mud puddle and make ripples with rocks. I want to think M&M's are better than money because you can eat them. I want to lie under a big oak tree and run a lemonade stand with my friends on a hot summer day. I want to return to a time when life was simple.
>
> When all you knew were colors, multiplication tables, and nursery rhymes, but that didn't bother you because you didn't know what you didn't know and you didn't care. All you knew was to be happy, and you were blissfully unaware of all things that should make you worried or upset. I want to think the world is fair. That everyone is honest and good.
>
> I want to believe that anything is possible. I want to be oblivious to the complexities of life and be overly excited by little things again. I want to live simple again. I don't want my day to consist of computer crashes, mountains of paperwork, how to survive more days in the month than there is money in the bank, doctors bills, gossip, illness, and loss of loved ones. I want to believe in the power of smiles, hugs, a kind word, truth, justice, peace, dreams, the imagination, mankind, and making angels in the snow.
>
> So . . . here's my checkbook and my car keys, my credit card bills, and my 401K statements. I am officially resigning from adulthood. And if you want to discuss this further, you'll have to catch me first, 'cause
>
> TAG!
> You're it!

Chapter Thirty-Eight

Another thing I cherish is humor. I have every one of Dave Barry's books. I've read both Woody and Steve Allen. I love Mark Twain, P.G. Wodehouse, Robert Benchley, and James Thurber. George Carlin, Jonathan Winters, Richard Pryor, and Robin Williams crack me up, as do many other stand-up comics. I marvel at the way Red Skelton and Jackie Gleason skated the thin line between comedy and tragedy. Billy Crystal and Whoopi Goldberg are more mod-
comedians who do that excellently. I can be equally
ained by the mad antics of the Marx brothers and the
room comedy of Noel Coward. Practically the only
tch on television is comedy, and the only part of
er I truly enjoy is the comics. A lump formed in
n Charles Schultz died.
n absolute essential in my life.
als who make us laugh are great, but I
stuff that happens to each of us every
say and do every day that is silly,
uous, stupid, outrageous, witty or
akes us laugh or at least, smile.
arriage is that both Mary and I

laugh easily with each other. That's a key factor in all my relationships.

A couple weeks ago, I was browsing in the humor section of a Barnes and Noble, and I picked up a book called *The Stupidest Things Ever Said by Politicians*. I resisted buying it (so far) assuming it would mostly be Dan Quayle quotes anyway. But I got thinking about some of the stupid things people have said to me and, in some cases, my absolutely brilliant and witty responses. (Their version of the same incident: I asked a perfectly innocent question and this old geezer said the stupidest thing.)

When I was in high school, I had a friend who called me nearly every day. He'd call me at home, at the cab office when I was working, at the pool hall where I hung out, or at another friend's house. It made no difference where he would happen to find me, the first words out of his mouth when I answered would be, "Hello Bob, where you at?"

The stupidity of that question pales in comparison to the one my grandmother asked me several times a day: "Do you want a spanking?" You'd think that through the generations of parents who have asked that question somehow they would have figured out that it's a rather dumb thing to ask. It's probably the all-time dumb question. What kind of response is expected? "Sure, Grandma. Why don't you just beat on me until you've worked out all your aggressions."

I was pretty much raised by my grandma until I was about eight, so I remember a couple more of her pet expressions. Whenever I was seeking comfort because of someone hurting my feelings, I remember her telling me, "That's okay. Five years from now you won't even remember this." It was well-meaning, and she was one hundred percent accurate. But I never found solace in those words. If my best friend had just told me he didn't want to be my friend anymore, I was hurting *right now*. Five years hence was beyond my comprehension. I needed something to make me feel better. NOW.

Like a cookie.

Grandma was also the one (and every family has this person) who was always giving me another think whenever

I was thinking, apparently, wrong. "Well, if that's what you think, young man, you've got another think coming." I'm not sure I ever did use up all my thinks. I may still have a few coming.

Perhaps it's because Grandma gave me all those thinks that I had teachers who used to ask, "Are you trying to get smart with me?" Dad used to tell me not to get smart with him. Come to think about it (I just used up one of Grandma's gift thinks), Mom did too. Nobody wanted me to get smart. And they thought I would never live up to their expectations.

The comedian, David Brenner, used to tell a great story about a stupid question a stranger asked him one day in Philadelphia. I was actually asked the same question one day in a mall in St. Cloud, Minnesota. When I tell the story I always acknowledge that I wish I had had the presence of mind to respond the way Mr. Brenner says he did. Mary and I had gone shopping. I finished before her and sat down on a bench to wait and do some serious people-watching. I had inadvertently sat on a newspaper. In a few minutes, an older gentleman approached. "Excuse me," he politely asked, "are you reading that paper?" Maybe it was the same guy Brenner had encountered in Philadelphia. What Brenner did was absolute genius. "Yes I am," he answered. Then he stood up, turned, picked up the paper, turned the page, set it down, and sat back down on it.

If I were that quick maybe I would come up with something really clever when someone asks, while I'm standing beneath a huge clock in a mall, "Do you know what time it is?" And I'd dearly love to have a snappy retort for all those folks who ask, "Is it hot (cold) enough for you?" when it's either ninety-five or thirty below. I certainly wish I had been that quick when I was seven or eight and someone told me to "act my age" or "quit crying or I'll give you something to cry about" and I already had something to cry about, thank you.

One day Mary and I were in a local restaurant, and she ordered a toasted cheese sandwich. After taking a couple steps toward the kitchen, the waitress turned and asked,

"Do you want the bread toasted?" As opposed to what? The plate? Pickles? The cheese? Maybe that waitress was related to the men's clothing store clerk who approached me while I was browsing in sportswear and said, "We have new jogging suits in your size, sir." Being sixty plus and weighing over two-fifty prompted me to stare at him and ask, "Why?"

That wasn't really a stupid question he asked. He was just trying to make a sale. So let's just call it a segue for the next story—one of my all-time favorite memories. At the conclusion of a weekend retreat near Marquette, Michigan, a group of us decided to stop at a restaurant in Bruce Crossing for dinner. There were about twelve of us in the group, and we had just shared a natural high that left us both happy and giddy. It was the silliness we took into the cafe. It was mid-afternoon, and we nearly had the place to ourselves. We put a couple tables together so we could all sit together. We were laughing and talking as the waitress took our orders. She joined in the fun and seemed to be enjoying the banter. We gave her a bit of a bad time, and she responded in kind. She was marvelous. As she prepared Charles King's salad at the salad bar, he began shouting instructions on not only what he wanted but exactly where she should place certain vegetables. When it dawned on her that he was directing her to build a face with cherry tomato eyes, a cucumber nose, and a carrot stick mouth she just hooted, as did the rest of us. We were all having a great time.

When she served the meals, she started with the lady on my left and proceeded clockwise around the group leaving my meal the last one delivered. As she set my plate down, she scanned our little party and asked, "Have I forgotten anything?"

I looked up at her and answered with my own question, "I don't know, what's the capital of North Dakota?" Instant pandemonium. Primed as were by our silly mood, we erupted as one in peals of laughter. I have no idea what the waitress said. I have no idea what anyone else said the rest of the afternoon. I have no idea what has happened to many of those folks. I don't even know how I got from where I started this chapter to this story—or where to go from here.

I think I'll quit.

Chapter Thirty-Nine

Modern technology has caused me to imagine the following phone call:

RING . . . RING . . . click.

"Good afternoon. Thank you for calling the Joseph L. Gooch Airline and Fertilizer Company. Our brand new automated answering service will now swiftly and conveniently accommodate your phone call: If you wish to check arrival or departure dates for any domestic flight, press 1 now. If you wish to confirm a reservation, press 2 now. If you wish a catalog of our latest fertilizers, press 3 now. If you are obsessive-compulsive, please press 4 over and over and over again."

I pressed 2.

"Thank you for using our brand new automated and super-efficient answering service. If you want to confirm a flight to New York, press 1 now. If you want to confirm a reservation for Chicago, press 2468 now. If you want to confirm a reservation for any other city east of the Mississippi, press E-A-S-T-O-F-M-I-S-S now. If you wish to confirm a reservation for a city between Minneapolis and Denver, press 3825968 now. If you wish to confirm a reservation for a city elsewhere, press 2 now. If you are extremely co-dependent, go press 2 for all your neighbors."

I was flying to California, so I pressed 2.

"Thank you for using our brand new automated answering service. Your satisfaction is very important to us. If you are confirming a reservation for either Los Angeles or San Francisco, press 1 now. If you are confirming a reservation for any other Northern California city press any other Northern California city now. If you are confirming another Southern California city flight, press S-C now."

My destination was San Diego so I pressed S-C.

"Thank you. Your call is really important to us but all our operators are busy helping other dazed and totally confused customers at present. Should you happen to be paranoid please consider that this call is probably being monitored. Please hold."

I wait. Country Western music begins to play. Bad country western music. Billy Ray Cyrus. Billy was interrupted every ten seconds by this syrupy voice advising me, "We apologize for the delay in answering your call. All of our agents are busy at the moment angering other customers, who are also very important to us. Please continue to hold, and your call will be attended to in the order in which it was received."

I wait. I listen to Billy Ray sing about his achy breaky hangnails. I listen to each interruption. Billy Ray is followed by Buck Owens and then Furlin Husky. They too were interrupted by the voice telling me how important I and my satisfaction were. This pattern was mercifully halted by another voice, this one sounded as if it were attached to a head, a whole entire body even. "How may I be of service this morning?" the voice asked.

It had to be a real person. A machine wouldn't know A.M. from P.M. "Thank you, sir. Thank you for being real. Thank you for actually conversing with me. We can have a real conversation can't we—you know, an exchange of ideas?"

"Of course we can. You know our goal is to please all our customers. Each and every one of you is very important to us. Now, how may I help you?"

164

"I'm calling about my upcoming flight to San Diego."

"Of course, sir. At the tone just punch in the eighteen digits of your flight number. You'll find them in the extremely faint lettering on page three of your itinerary. In the bottom right-hand corner. You have a nice day. Oh, and by the way, good luck."

A pregnant silence.

Beep.

Luckily I had anticipated the need for my flight number. I've dealt with these people before. I pressed the mumbers— all eighteen of them.

"Thank you for using our super-fast and efficient phone service that has been installed so that our company could downsize personnel in order to make more money for our stockholders while, at the same time, causing considerable inconvenience to you, our treasured customers, who are, after all, very important to us. Unfortunately the few remaining agents are busy talking with other disgruntled, but valued, customers. We apologize for the delay. Please hold. Your call will be answered in the order in which it was received."

Roy Clark. Grandpa Jones. The Haggars. The whole Hee Haw gang (minus the jokes and sexy girls) was, somehow, inside my telephone. Like clockwork, however, came the ten second reminders:

"Please hold. All of our agents are busy. . . ."

"Remember to ask our representative about our frequent. . . ."

"While you are waiting you might consider playing chess or watching *Titanic.*"

I was trapped. I was being held hostage by my own telephone. If I hang up now I'll have to call back and start the process all over. I can't do that. I've got to hang in there. It can't be much longer now. But how long can I stand this? Little voices continue talking to me. It doesn't really matter which numbers I push. No one is ever going to talk to me. Not now. Not ever. . . .

Chapter Forty-One

I overslept one morning, stubbed my toe as I stumbled into the bathroom, popped a button off my shirt as I was hurrying to dress, burned my toast, and, when I finally got in the car, ready to roll, it didn't start. Being the keenly perceptive person I am, I thought, "This is probably not going to be a good day. Maybe my bio-rhythms are out of whack or the planets aren't in the proper alignment of the charkras being feng shuied."

The truth is that some days, despite our best efforts and intentions, are simply not going to go well. Perhaps we are tired or not feeling well. Maybe we are out of sorts or preoccupied with a pressing matter and, thus, not giving our full attention to matters at hand. Maybe your moon is rising in the wrong house. Possibly you just got up on the wrong side of the bed. (Which is the right side anyway?) A key thing to remember when you are having one of those days is to indentify it for what it is. A bad day is just that—a bad day.

We don't need to compound it by giving in to our worst attitudes and behaviors. A bad day doesn't mean we are bad folks. The world is not against you. And it certainly doesn't mean it's the start of a bad week or month. It doesn't even

166

mean tomorrow will be a bad day too. It just means that today doesn't happen to be going so well. If you don't give the situation a lot of thought you just might be able to turn the day around before it's over.

We really are pretty much in control of what kind of day we will have. Each of us is free to see what we want to see, think what we want to think, and feel what we want to feel. To be sure, there is much that is outside your sphere of influence but you can choose how you will react toward those circumstances. They are, after all, your days. You can choose your attitude for the day. You can't blame someone else for the events of your life. Each of us has the responsiblity to determine his own fate.

When the wheels seem to be coming off, perhaps you need to slow down or take a time out. Take a milk and cookies break—for a really long time. You may need to be still and/or let go, turn it over to a Higher Power. I used to be leery of surrender to a Higher Power until I realized I wasn't doing all that well on my own.

You may even discover there's a reason for your bad day. There might be a message for you, but you have to be alert—pay attention, listen—to get it. It may turn out that what's happening isn't so bad after all. When you let go, it frees you to search your experience for answers to deeper questions about yourself. Often when your out of sync, you need to discover what you need to do to get centered and back in harmony with yourself. It's progress you're after, not perfection. Use your bad experiences to help you see what you need to continue your progress. And have a good day.

To put this in perspective, let's examine what constitutes a good day. I used to be much more goal oriented than I am now. I tried impressing people, and I wanted to be successful. When things weren't working, I became more and more determined to make them work my way. I wanted to make more money. I wanted to play better golf. I wanted to look better. I wanted to "save" every kid I counseled. And I wanted to be such a great teacher. I wanted pearls of wisdom to continually drop from my lips so I could watch the students eagerly scrambling to catch them. I wanted every one to like me. I was a pretty good hero. And, as you would expect, I was constantly frustrated and disappointed in myself. Whatever I did was never good enough. I learned this message growing up, and I kept beating myself up with it as an adult.

I've gotten a lot healthier about this in the last twenty years, thanks to the several programs with which I've been involved and the people I've become friends with through those programs. One of the key pieces was something my dear friend Mark Storry (Book) said to me one day (and many times since), "If at first you don't succeed, lower your expectations." If I knew who Mark stole that line from, I'd gladly give him credit. If you are like me, you probably first read that as a negative. But think about. Most of us have these incredibly unrealistic expectations for ourselves and we want to achieve them all—RIGHT NOW. Of course we will fail. What this statement really means is to cut yourself some slack; be a little more gentle with yourself.

My formula for a good day is now much simpler. Given my health and trauma history, I consider it a good day if I don't get cancer, divorced, or have a heart attack. Perhaps that is a little too simple for you. Here's one that is a little more practical and applies to everyone. This was E-mailed to me by Book's brother, Paul. It was titled "Life's Prescription," and it reads.

1. Show up
2. Pay attention
3. Do your best
4. Let go of the results

I figure if I can go to bed knowing I did those those four things it was a good day.

"Everybody thinks of
changing humanity
and nobody thinks of
changing himself."
—Leo Tolstoy

"The real voyage of
discovery consists not
in seeking new lands,
but in seeing with
new eyes."
—Marcel Proust

Chapter Forty-One

In 1978 I attended a workshop in Minneapolis presented by Virginia Satir, the author of *Peoplemaking* and one of my all-time heroes. When she talks or writes about human behavior she makes more sense to me than anyone else in the field. I was in awe of how masterfully she presented her material and handled herself on stage. She did intimate family therapy in front of several hundred people. It was amazing to watch and wonderful to experience. A small part of that seminar was a presentation on perception that was to become a lynch pin for my counseling career. I happen to believe that understanding perception is the key to understanding people—if you can see through the eyes of the other, you understand. It's that simple. Ms. Satir's viewpoint strengthened that belief, and I adopted her outline as a teaching (and learning) tool.

The lecture was divided into four parts: the way we view relationships, the way we view people, how we explain events, and how we view change. First she presented how she believed our society perceives these four and then how the world might change if we would choose to alter those perceptions. I have put this basic concept into my own frame of reference and have used it for both classroom lectures and workshop presentations of my own. I think it is as relevant today as it was nearly a quarter century ago. Some basic truths don't change.

I offer this in the same format as Ms. Satir did. First I will cover how I feel the world has been operating the past fifty years or so and then switch to how it might be if we could learn a new point of view regarding these four elements of life.

The first question is: How do we view relationships? Ms. Satir's answer was (is) that we perceive the way we relate to one another in terms of hierarchies—that one person has more power in the relationship. Most organizations are easy to identify in this light. A school is a good example. The hierarchy looks like this: School board, superintendent, lesser administrators, i.e., principals and deans, teaching faculty, auxiliary staff i.e., secretaries, custodians and cooks, and students. (I know parents should be at the top of this list, but the reality is that schools function similarly to other organizations in that the governing body pays precious little attention to the people they represent.) The government, businesses, churches, and families function, to various degrees, in a hierarchal fashion too. It's the American way. I'm not trying to be critical here. (That would be too easy actually.) I'm merely describing the social order we have established.

Into that system I want to project what might be an unlikely scenario—or not. I need something dramatic for effect. Feel free to insert your own example. Unfortunately a lot of life experiences fit quite nicely. Back to our school. A teacher is pretty certain he spots one of his students, a not-so-good scholar, cheating on a rather important test. Let's be clear about this. The boy is not cheating. The teacher, for whatever reason (past history, the boy's furtive look, whatever), thinks he is. It is a matter of perception. The teacher walks over to the student's desk, picks up his test paper, and rips it up, saying, "I don't tolerate cheating in my class."

Imagine you are the boy. How do you feel about this incident right now? You protest. The situation escalates, and the teacher sends you to the office because of your insolence. You stomp down to the principal's office and tell him what happened. The principal manages to get you calmed down and then asks the teacher to join the two of you. The teacher insists he saw you cheating. There is no doubt in his mind. You insist you weren't cheating. Who is the principal most likely, almost certainly, going to support? How does that make you feel? Principals tell their teachers in workshops that they can count on him backing them up. It is necessary if he is to establish his credibility with his faculty. He is, as a matter-of-fact, likely to publicly back the teacher even when he believes the student. You go up the ladder with similar results. The superintendent backs the principal, and the school board backs the superintendent.

That's the way a hierarchy works. The people at the top are farthest removed from the day-to-day operations and know the least about what actually goes on in the trenches. And yet they wield all the power. The further down the chain of command you are the more frustrated, angry, resentful, and powerless you feel. The social structure that has evolved reflects the same thought process and people, perhaps unconsciously, are placed (and place themselves) in that structure according to wealth, occupation, race, and other external factors. The result is the same sort of resentment and powerlessness from those perceived in the lowest social positions.

Now let's look at the second question. How do we see individuals? In every demographic we have carefully created ways in which people are "supposed" to be and the closer they conform to the established norms the more acceptable they are. The key word is conformity. We perceive people according to how closely they conform to our standards—and we all have different standards. Picture yurself in a busy mall. Strolling down the corridor is a young boy with green, spiked hair. He's wearing baggy shorts, the kind with the crotch at his knees, untied sneakers, and a tee-shirt emblazoned with a skull and crossbones. He has a stud in his pierced nose and a dog collar around his neck. Before he reaches the end of the lane he will probably be perceived as, among other things, weird, scary, really cool, stupid, and perfectly normal. Too easy? How about the twenty-somerthing young man with glasses, pleated slacks, a button-down shirt, a tie, and highly polished black oxfords. Mightn't he be considered by various people as handsome, gay, a nerd, an uptight sales associate, or a junior executive.

The point is we tend to think in stereotypes, put labels on folks to make them manageable, and have our own rules about what is acceptable, okay, and/or normal. We are all trying to fit into one or more groups so we adapt our behaviors to fit the standards of each group. How well we are accepted by the group is determined by how closely we conform to those norms. When we don't fit in we feel inadequate, inferior, envious, and resentful. We tend to interpret there is something wrong with us—that somehow, we have failed.

Ms. Satir's third question is: How do we explain events? Ever since the Age of Reason, at least, we have pretty much explained things in a linear manner. A causes B. We expect things to be logical, sequential, and binary. That may work well in the physical world but when considering human behavior it leads to a lot of blame and shame, control, manipulation, and duality of thought. If everything is cause and effect there has to be someone to blame if things go wrong. That creates a ton of guilt feelings in many people. Shades of gray are hard to acknowledge in a black or white world of polarities—up/down, male/female, right/wrong, Republican/Democrat, win/lose and all other manner of dualities. Linear thinking leads us to suffer from the illusion of control. We tend to think we either can or should control people and things which prompts us to be manipulative, duplicitous and use reward and punishment as motivation. The result is a lot of folks who feel used, are angry, and filled with guilt and shame.

172

Finally, we ask, how do we view change? There is a simple answer. We don't like it, we don't want it, and we resist it with every fiber of our being. We defend and fight to maintain the status quo. In nearly every area of our lives, we want things to stay the same—predictable, familiar, stable and dependable. It is so much more simple when things are static. There's no need to question. No need to think. After all if "it was good enough for . . ." or "it's always been this way" then it surely must be good enough. Since things are always in flux and change constantly this need for constancy and the security that provides leaves many feeling fearful of their world.

What I've described in this chapter isn't pretty. It is, however, the dysfunctional system that has been in place for generations. It's a dishonest system—a system where we find it difficult to admit not knowing something. We can't, or won't admit making a mistake. It leads to unhealthy relationships within the system, which, in turn, helps perpetuate the system. It has become a way of life primarily motivated by fear, accompanied by resentment, anger, guilt and shame, feelings of inadequacy, feeling alienated and disconnected, and a sense of powerlessness. Look at the problems we identify in our society—crime, racism, drug and alcohol abuse, apathy, hate crimes, broken families, homelessness, whatever. The causes for each are the feelings I've just described. The problems we face are the ones created by the system we have developed. And we are afraid.

We are afraid to change.

Ironically any answers or solutions will be found only when we find the courage to change. "If you always do what you always did, you will always get what you always got." (I'd love to credit the author of that statement, but I have no idea what the original source is. Thank you, whoever you are.) What Ms. Satir proposed and I support is going to sound like John Lennon singing "Imagine"—a little pie in the sky, looking at the world through rose-colored glasses sort of thing. But it is simply a variation of what many great theologians, philosophers, and humanitarians have suggested for thousands of years. It is what Christ taught. And Buddha. And Lao-Tze. And Muhammed. It involves a shift in perception regarding the four questions addressed by this outline.

What if, instead of hierarchical thinking, we really viewed all our relationships in terms of equality. Everyone is of equal value to everyone else. Each of us no better than anyone else; and no worse. No one is more important. We have paid lip-service to this idea for thousands of years, but we've never really practiced it. As you read this, you are probably thinking to yourself, "Well I think everyone is equal." I suspect most people in the world would say that. But something's wrong because we are still killing each other. There are still thousands of homeless and starving people. Racism is as bad in this millennium as it was in the last two. Countries still go to war over religious beliefs and property disputes. There is still something very wrong with the way we view the various relationships among people.

Another concept we pay great lip-service to is the uniqueness of each individual. Think of the huge change in society if we actually did honor and respect the beautiful diversity among the people on this planet—if we actually celebrated the magic of each individual and cherished the multitude of colors and beliefs that populate this world. What if there were no arbitrary standards of dress and behavior folks had to conform to just to find acceptance by their peers. Look around. We have created the United States of Generica.

And what if we explained events in a more synergistic way—if we explore the nuances and shades of gray instead of compartmentalizing everything into nice, neat, tiny little boxes? What if we didn't need a scapegoat if things go awry? Why does there have to be someone at fault all the time? "Shit happens" was a popular slogan a few years ago. We thought it was funny. But it is also true. Most stuff just happens. There is no need to blame someone. It just happens. What if, instead of finding fault and laying blame, we looked for solutions? Can you imagine the change that could bring in politics alone?

174

And what if we looked at change as desirable rather than something to be feared? Can't change just as easily be viewed as adding something to your life as it is taking something away? You can see change as an exciting challenge, something adding zest to your life. Put change in perspective. Compare your life today with the way life was the day you were born and you are almost certain to see the good that can come from change. Each of the things you can identify as an improvement was probably once feared by those who came ahead of you. Change is ineviable. Change is the one constant in our lives. You can relax and enjoy the view just as easily as you can fear it. It makes the trip more fun.

Forgive me if this sounds like a soap-box oration. Maybe it's the pain I've witnessed in the lives of the thousands of kids I've worked with, but I am tired of seeing people hurt each other. I don't like to see folks burdened with the load of hurt, guilt, fear, shame, resentment, and anger our addictive society doles out in large measures. Maybe I am a Pollyanna, or as a good friend once affectionately called me, "one of those touchy-feely sons-of-bitches," but I think we can make things better.

You may not agree with any of the concepts in this chapter (why do you think I put it near the end?) and it may be a huge dream, but what if each one of us just shifted his/her perception a little bit and made a slight adjustment in the way we treat some folks?

What if . . . ?

Chapter Forty-Two

The first quote on this page is a lyric from "The Magic Song" written at the very first PIP camp back in 1984. The first time Mark sang it I cried like a baby because he claimed I inspired the song with a talk I had given earlier in the year and he dedicated the song to me. I had never considered myself the source of inspiration for anything and I'd never had anything dedicated to me (except a couple of year-books.) I was deeply touched by this most generous honor. Especially when I consider the wonderfully affirming lyric:
"What is the magic, the secret ingredient that makes all
        this happen, that changes our lives?
What special power ascends or descends
        what mystical magic moves you to be moved?
Well, I know the answer. If you'll listen I'll tell you—
        the magic is you.
Listen the secret is you. Listen the power's in you.
        Listen, please listen, the magic is you."

That, my dear friends, is the most powerful message I can give you—the simple fact that you are the magic. You are the magic. Our personal power is awesome. We have complete control of our perceptions. we determine our own attitudes. This is what makes things happen and effects change in our lives. We need to recognize this power we have. We need to use it. To rely on it. Using this magic is what will make it possible to change the perceptions suggested in the last chapter. We are responsible for determining our own fate. And we have everything we need to make it happen. Viktor Frankl wrote in Man's Search for Meaning, ". . . everything can be taken from a man except one thing: the last of the human freedoms—to choose one's attitude in any given set of circumstances, to choose one's own way . . ." The full impact of Frankl's words lies in the realization that he was writing from a Nazi concentration camp during World War II. Read the quote again with the picture of a death camp in your mind. Read it a couple times. Let it sink in—deep.

No matter the circumstances we have the freedom to choose our own way. We can choose how we will live our lives. It is important to note that choosing very often means taking risks. The more at stake the greater the risk. Somewhere along the way we may have to unlearn some old behaviors and learn new ways of thinking and doing. You are capable of learning new ways and you are capable of taking the necessary risks. "Real courage," Tom Robbins once wrote, "is risking something you have to keep on living with . . ." There are five risks I feel are necessary, risks that take real courage, if you want to experience the full impact of freedom and love.

First is to risk choosing to like yourself. That sounds so simple but many folks seem to have a great deal of difficulty accepting themselves as they are. I believe we are born with an innate sense of self-worth and love but that good feeling about ourselves slowly erodes as our environment expands and we cross paths of more and more people. So many well-meaning people, in their efforts to teach or discipline inadvertently chip away at our self-image. And then there are our detractors who assault us with insult and innuendo. We listen. We learn. We block out the positive and internalize the negative resulting in a ton of self-doubt and feelings of inadequacy. The bulk of our self talk becomes negative. We insist on remembering every mistake we ever made and pointing out every flaw in our character and/or body. We attempt to conform and invoke upon ourselves the rule of too . . . "I'm too fat."

"My hair is too straight."

"My feet are too big."

"My boobs are too small."

"I'm too short."

"I'm too dumb."

Those are lies you are telling yourself. Who you are, how you were created, is somebody special, wonderful, unique, lovable, and imperfect. That's who you are. That's the magic of you. Anybody, including yourself, who tells you something other than how special, wonderful, unique and lovable you are is lying to you. You have the power to choose. Don't listen to the lies. Do you think Viktor Frankl listened to what his Nazi detractors said about him? You can choose your attitude in any set of circumstances. Choose to talk nice to yourself. Choose to like yourself.

And you can like other people too. You can choose to risk accepting others at face value. You can choose to quit playing the games society dictates. You can ignore the rules for conformity your group(s) sets up and decide for yourself the merits of each other person in your life. There is something to value and cherish in everyone and you can find that if you choose to look. But you have to set aside all the labels. Folks don't have to be worthy of your love and acceptance. Like you, they just have to be themselves. They just have to be—with whatever faults, blemishes, and weaknesses may have come with the package. You can choose to love them. We all share the same world and we have far more in common with folks than whatever the surface suggests. We have the same feelings. We all know joy, sadness, excitement, guilt, grief, anger, and the whole gamut of emotions. Set aside the labels. Labels isolate and alienate. Labels give us permission to not look at individuals. You can learn to look at folks as individuals.

Thirdly, I believe we need to risk living for today. Meaning doesn't exist in the past or the future and neither do you. Who you are is who you are today. It has been said we crucify ourselves between two thieves—yesterday and tomorrow. They rob us of today. Risk to live in the moment. Jules Renard summed up this concept beautifully. " If I were to begin life again," he wrote in *The Journal of Jules Renard*, "I should want it as it was. I would only open my eyes a little more." We need to show up and pay attention. It's that simple. The nicest feeling Mary and I share as a married couple is simply being there. You get so much more from each moment when you are fully present—in the moment. The best guarantee of a happy tomorrow is to be fully present and get the most from today. You have the power to make that choice.

A fourth risk is to risk choosing to be spontaneous. Being spontaneous is pretty much a matter of giving yourself permission. It is giving yourself permission to have fun. Tilt the world a little. Change your perception. If you are depressed about something ask yourself how a four-year-old would view the same thing. Look for the absurdity that abounds in our world. There is so much that makes so little sense. Instead of letting that absurdity upset you choose to adapt the attitude displayed on the TV show, M*A*S*H. Let the madness escape in little, harmless doses. Make your workplace (school, home, institution) fun again. Us Geezers remember when it was truly fun to go to work. You can also choose to give yourself permission to feel your feelings. It is through our feelings we are able to really connect with people. Our feelings give depth and meaning to everything else. We truly experience the world through our hearts.

And finally I think we have to risk choosing not to be afraid. I think this means risking to choose for a higher power, a belief in the mystery. For me, it is the only way I can explain things that are totally beyond my understanding and totally unexplainable.When a loved one commits suicide, when a toddler's life is snuffed out, when someone is born crippled or retarded I can't handle that alone. I can only handle a great tragedy by accepting, not only that I can't handle it, but I can't even comprehend it. My spirituality includes all that I don't understand. That's a lot. I am absolutely convinced Somebody up there likes me. Because of that I have absolutely nothing to fear.

If you really want to be free you have to take some risks. The greatest risk of all is to risk nothing. By not risking you stay stuck. Only the person willing to take reasonable risks is free to make and accept change. Only the person willing to take risks is free to love. You have the power (the magic is you) to risk.

The choice is yours.

"You have to live life
to love life.
And you have to love
life to live life.
It's a vicious circle."
—Unknown

"Some people walk
in the rain.
Others just get wet."
—Roger Miller

Chapter Forty-Three

Every Christmas season when I watch Frank Capra's *It's a Wonderful Life,* I choke up when the folks of Bedford Falls begin arriving at the Bailey house. By the time Clarence gets his wings, tears are streaming profusely down my cheeks. I can't control it. It's not just that I'm a softy who likes that sappy stuff but it's also because I identify with George Bailey. Oh, I've never saved the life of a hero to be or kept the town miser at bay so the town folk could eke out a living and have a decent place to live. But I believe—I have no doubt—that if I were ever in serious trouble my friends would show up in droves from all over to help out. The ones who couldn't make it would call to let me know they were thinking of me. In 1983 I actually did have about three hundred people show up at a local school board meeting to show support for me and the counseling and guidance program.

I too have had a wonderful life. Like Lou Gehrig, "I consider myself the luckiest man on the face of the earth." I have been thinking a lot lately about how richly my life has been blessed and I'd like to share some of those thoughts. As I write this I am sitting in my cabin at PIP camp near Virginia, Minnesota. One of the things that just occurred to

181

me is that PIP embodies all of what I consider the essential ingredients of my wonderful life. PIP stands for Partner in Prevention and is dedicated to helping kids create healthier life styles for themselves. I've been involved since 1982 and have seen thousands of young people come alive socially, emotionally, volitionally, intellectually, and spiritually. More to the task at hand, that same thing has happened for me, proving for me, beyond any doubt, that what you give away comes back to you a hundredfold.

When I do my do my daily meditations I express thanks for four areas of my life—the gifts I've been given, the cast of characters on my journey, the experiences I've had, and the opportunites that have been presented to me. PIP has been one of those opportunities, an opportunity to share my gifts, associate with the best friends I've ever had (and meet new ones at each event), and to experience some of the most wonderful moments of my life. (If you've ever been "whooooshed" by nearly a hundred people you know what a great feeling it is. [Private joke for everyone who was at camp in 2000]) I can't begin to express my gratitude to the folks who started and those who have helped maintain this program because it has been an integral part of my life from the moment I got involved. It has helped change me in so many positive ways and I now consider myself a better husband, father, grandfather, teacher, counselor, and friend than ever.

That said, I want to wrap this book up by elaborating a little on those four areas I mentioned to help you better understand why I consider myself so lucky and to have had such an absolutely wonderful life. It's not easy to separate the four as they are inexorably woven together to form the tapestry of my life. The total adds up to who I have become—who I am at this moment. I am happy with that outcome.

I believe I have been blessed with countless gifts, gifts I treasure dearly and for which I give daily thanks. I could not have fashioned this life without the abundance my Higher Power has bestowed upon me. I have often expressed that, as I have traveled my journey, I have paid attention. Doing so is, perhaps, my greatest strength. Had I been less alert I would have learned less, consequently I would have had less to give back. I think I was given above-average intelligence but that, in and of itself, is grossly overrated. It's applying what you know that makes a difference. Knowledge, understanding, and all that other head stuff is fine but if you don't do anything with it it has precious little value. If you are unaware of what is going on around you and unable to see how things relate to one another the knowledge is wasted.

I have been blessed with good language skills. I read well and that enables me to learn anything and everything I choose. It's all written down somewhere. I am a good listener and that allows me learn from the people in my life. These two gifts give me an unlimited capacity to learn. And my speaking and writing skills provide me with the means to give it all back.

I have been given the capacity to care deeply about people. Whatever success I've had as a counselor/educator and as a friend has been because I genuinely care about the folks I know—all of them. I can love both easily and unconditionaly. Forgiveness comes readily for me. Empathy is second nature. I find it relatively effortless to place myself in another's shoes, to see and feel what they see and feel. I don't make judgements. It's not my job. Nor does it interest me. I readily see the good in people. Being kind seems to come naturally. In short, I have been blessed with a big heart and I treat the hearts of others with gentleness.

The final gift I want to mention is my sense of humor. I love the way my mind is able to tilt the world enough to find the incongruities in the way we are. I have the M*A*S*H* attitude I mentioned in the last chapter, finding the humor even in the most dire circumstances. I can see the world with loving irreverence. I laugh easily at myself and I'm not afraid to look foolish. Letting out the child in me is a skill I have acquired. Besides making life more enjoyable and fun, the sense of humor with which I've been blessed has made it much easier to cope.

The gifts can be enjoyed intrinsically but what makes my

life all the more special is that I have been given the opportunity to share, to give back, all the gifts. I was afforded the opportunity to spend my life with young people, first as a teacher and then as a counselor, both in the school and in about two hundred PIPfests and similar events. I figure I've had the opportunity to meet nearly thirty thousand young people. I can't imagine a career with more rewards than that of an educator. The knowledge imparted in the classroom is incidental. What you really do is touch lives. The influence and reach of a teacher is limitless. And I found, as a counselor, the experience was even more intimate and powerful. I got to work with kids on a one-to-one basis and the agenda for our sessions was theirs, not mine (or a curriculum director's). We talked about what the student needed rather than what I thought they needed. That's a huge difference. I've been able to give back gifts as a speaker and as a writer. Both have offered me the opportunity to reach wider audiences.

The third area of gratitude is the wide range of experiences I've had. As I look back at the panorama of my life I realize the truth of the Taoist story I told in *It's So Simple . . . It Just Ain't Easy*—the one about the old man who kept asking, "How do you know?" whenever a friend judged an experience as either good or bad. I believe every experience is merely that—an experience. To make judgements about or try to quantify an experience diminishes its depth. Earlier I wrote about how unhappy I was babysitting my little sister when I was a teenager and how that turned out to be a huge blessing in raising my own kids and the basis for the wonderful relationship I have always had with my sister. I could say similar things about my divorce, my cancer, and my heart attack. Peter G. Peterson, whoever he is, once wrote, "The experience may have been costly, but it was also priceless." There is a gift in each and every experience. It is the Yin/Yang of life. Part of the mystery.

And finally I am grateful for the people who have populated my life. All of them. Each and every one. Each is, to some degree or other, a part of who I am. Each has impacted on me in some way—contributed to my life's experience. I have shared rather extensively with my readers my immediate family. My eternal thanks to my parents was expressed in Chapter One of the first book. My brother Jack and sister Joy have been lifelong friends and I love them both dearly. My grandparents and two cousins Don Kittell and Marian Korterud were other very positive influences in my growing up years. And I am forever in debt to Marian's brother, Tom, who introduced me to golf.

I've been married to two wonderful women, each of whom was just the person I most needed at the respective periods of my life. My natural children, Jodi and Mark, are the dearest friends I have and I am very proud to say I have had a great relationship with each throughout their lives. Mary's son Troy and our foster daughter Becky each stepped in at the right time to fill in the huge void left by Jodi and Mark moving out on their own. I love them both dearly and consider them good friends too. I think the thing I've done best in my life is to be dad. In both these marriages I got some wonderful in-laws too. Rapidly rising to the top of my relationship list are my two grandchildren, Megan and Jordan. I so wish I could spend more time with them but time/distance is a huge factor. It's comforting to know they both have special places in my heart and when I need to be with either, I can go to that place and they are always there.

I have had such a marvelous family. And most marvelous friends too. At the risk of offending some others I want to express my deep affection for Mark Storry and Barb Elseth, the two friends who have been there for me during the darkest moments of the past twenty years. And Don Anderson, who was the first friend I made in Paynesville and is still my best local friend. And there is, of course, my PIP family—Jim Grzeskowiak, Dave Sjoblad, Dave Buker, Charles King, Tom Keating, Bernie Nelson and all the others. There are too many co-workers and friends to mention. And I have to mention the thousands of kids who have trusted me with their most intimate secrets. As I write this I find myself being caught up in the same feelings I have when I watch the movie. I am overwhelmed. I am stunned. I am totally humbled by being blessed with so very many people in my life. I could probably write another book just about people.

But I'm not going to.

As I cap this off I'm completely blown away with what has been a life so rich and joyful. I so often find myself wondering what I did to deserve so much. The only answer that makes any sense is nothing. It's all been a gift. A wonderful gift. Thank you.

It's been a wonderful life.

I can hardly wait to find out what's going to happen next.

Time Flies Whether You're Having Fun or Not
MAKES A WONDERFUL GIFT FOR:
People in recovery
Folks who know Bob
Former students and Pippers
People with a sense of humor
People who like people
Wounded healers
People in education or other helping professions
People who enjoy life and feel alive

....

To order additional copies of
Time Flies Whether You're Having Fun or Not
send a check or money order for $12.95
Please add $2.00 for shipping and handling;
Minnesota residents add 6.5% sales tax to:

Bob Cushman
705 Paine Drive
Paynesville, MN 56362

You can get a copy of Bob's first book,
It's So Simple . . . It Just Ain't Easy
by sending an additional $3.00,
includes shipping, handling, and tax,
as long as the limited supply lasts. 2 for $5.00.